CHEER UP!

A Guide to Success at Tryouts

Coach Lori

outskirts
press

Outskirts Press, Inc.
http://www.outskirtspress.com

ISBN: 978-1-9772-6323-0

Cover Photo © 2023 Lori Steffen. All rights reserved - used with permission.

Outskirts Press and the "OP" logo are trademarks belonging to Outskirts Press, Inc.

PRINTED IN THE UNITED STATES OF AMERICA

WARNING

This book is intended to provide information and education regarding proper cheer technique and practice. However, like all forms of exercise, many of the techniques associated with the sport of cheerleading can be dangerous, and if not performed properly, can result in serious injury or even death. It is important that readers know their limits and take responsibility for their own safety. If, after reading this book, you are in any way unsure about the safety of a cheer technique, it is important that you seek advice from an experienced cheerleading instructor before attempting the technique

Dedication

To my husband Mark and my daughters, Holly, and Robyn.

Thank you for your love, support, and most of all your patience.

Table of Contents

Introduction

You want to be a cheerleader? That's great! With some hard work, time, and determination, this guide will provide you with a plan to make that dream a reality! But it's up to you to follow the plan and do the work. Nothing worth having comes easy, and cheer is no exception.

While the advice found in the following pages provides a guide to becoming as ready as you can personally be for cheer tryouts, it does not guarantee success. So much of tryouts depends on outside factors for which you cannot compensate. Are the judges fair and impartial? Is the program's focus on a skill you are weak in? Will something happen in your life that throws you off on that critical day?

There are no guarantees that everything will go perfectly. The time that you spend on the tryouts floor is like a phone video, not a movie. The judges don't get to know you. They don't know if you're smart, or motivated or a great person. They are looking at your skills, your attitude, and your floor presence during the "snap-shot" of time during which you're in front of them. Make it count. Do your best to prepare, and then give them all you've got when you get your chance.

This book is a guide to help you learn and prepare. **No guarantees. No promises.** Just a good, sound plan to help you be as ready as you can personally be on tryouts day.

The emphasis is on **YOU**. **You** do the work. **You** put in the time. **You** perform at the top of your ability, and **You** may make the squad. But one thing is certain – **You won't make it if you don't try.**

So, let's get started!

CHAPTER I

In Gear to Cheer

Learning to cheer, you need the basic skills including well executed jumps, sharp and correctly placed motions, a loud voice that yells instead of screams, and floor presence that radiates confidence and excitement, that in turn excites the crowd. This book can help you achieve your best level of these skills if you do the work and follow the suggestions exactly. Don't cut corners, or do half the work, or pass on the awkward stuff. Some of it may feel really uncomfortable! You need to make the judges see you as a cheerleader before you can become one. Therefore, you must feel like one – or at least look like you do!

Try thinking of it this way: Tryouts are an audition, and you are trying to win a part. The judges will score you on skill and spirit, but they will also be judging your ability to engage the crowd. Do you come across as someone they want to see on the sidelines? Are you happy and excited, or so nervous you look ready to get sick? Are you neat and properly dressed, or in baggy clothes with your hair in your eyes? Do you seem confident and natural on the floor? If not, you aren't projecting the right impression, and it will count against you! Let's work together to be sure that when you step on that floor, you're ready in every way to win a place on the squad!

Some points to remember as you work through the book:

A. **Your brain is the laziest organ in your body.** It rides around in your head, cushioned and comfortable, telling the rest of your body what to do. If you allow it the path of least resistance, it will take it. It will allow your legs to only go halfway to the jump height. It will let your arms flop and reach down. Your brain controls motor skills and it is engineered to save energy and preserve the body until it recognizes danger or extreme need. Then the brain will engage and push your body to perform at a much higher level. Your conscious mind, housed within your brain, is a different story. This is the part of your brain that decides when that "extreme need" has come. You control what your mind tells your brain. Want your body to do the work? Your mind tells your brain to make it happen. Don't think you can do it? Your mind will tell your brain that too. How do you correct that? Tell yourself you can. Ever heard "confess it to possess it?" It's true. Commit this phrase to memory and use it.

> **"What your mouth says, your ears hear,
> your mind believes."**

Sound contradictory? Think about it. You're the smartest person your brain knows. You're the only one it listens to. It makes your body do whatever your mind tells it to. Say *out loud* that you can do the jump and you will. Say *out loud* that your jumps are going to get better? They will. Say, or even think, that they are terrible? They will be. You can build yourself up or tear yourself down. Choose to be your own best cheerleader. How do you expect someone else to believe your cheers if you don't believe them yourself?

B. **Every jump is two jumps, not one**. You jump up, and you jump back down. Your arms and legs must be actively involved in both directions. If you simply fall back to earth, your landing will reflect it. As with everything in life, you get out of it what you put into it.

C. **Falling when you land a jump won't kill you**. Barring unexpected physical issues that you may or may not have, blowing your landing won't kill you, it won't paralyze you, and you won't die. Don't believe me? How far is your butt from the ground? Bend your knees and sit down on the ground without catching yourself. Are you dead? Not likely. Losing your balance and catching yourself is usually the worst that will happen, but don't be stupid about it. Don't practice on gravel or broken glass. Don't even practice on concrete if you can help it (very hard on the knees over time...). Don't be afraid! Fear of landing will make your brain tell your legs not to go too high because they might not get back under you in time. It's ridiculous. Stop being afraid to jump! Put all your strength and power into it! No one ever flew off into the sky, never to return, from jumping high under their own effort. I promise.

D. **"I'm too shy to get up in front of people."** Then **WHY** on earth are you doing this?

> If your WHY isn't strong enough to overcome your fears,
> You need a NEW WHY.

There are many ways to overcome fear once you find a strong enough WHY. When something matters enough to you, you will find a way to face the obstacles. Afraid to get up in front of people? Do exactly that. Get out in front of people and do your jumps. Shout a cheer. Or actually shout, "I'm trying out for cheerleading and I need to conquer my fears!" You'll find out people either don't care what anyone else is doing, or it really doesn't matter what anyone else thinks. You'll still be you; you'll still be on track to tryout, and you will have done what you were afraid to do.

E. **Making Cheerleading won't instantly make you popular.**
If that's your "Why", great! But understand that it will take more than your name on a list to accomplish it.

And ask yourself, "Popular with who?" Who are you attempting to reach? Do you want to be part of a certain group that associates with the cheerleaders? Are you trying to get to the top of your current social circle? Or do you simply want to be a well-known name in your school?

Then be someone that everyone "**likes**" first, and someone that everyone **"sees"** second. Popularity is a double-edged sword, and it can be as painful as it is fun.

Be careful what you're popular for. Make it for always being the nicest person in the room who treats everyone like they're important! That way, at your ten-year reunion, when all these teenage concerns have faded, people will still be happy to see you, instead of secretly hoping you've been miserable.

CHAPTER 2

Words and Phrases

1: **Blades:**
Hand is flat, fingers straight and closed. Hand will naturally cup just slightly. Do not attempt to over straighten the hand. This will result in fingers arching backward in an awkward manner.

Horizontal Blade

Vertical Blade

2: **Body Clock:**

The Body Clock is my way of explaining where to turn or move parts of your own body. Think of yourself as a clock, with your feet as 6:00 and your head as 12:00. Your arms in "T" fall at 3 and 9. A low "V" will have you pointing your arms at approximately 5 and 7.

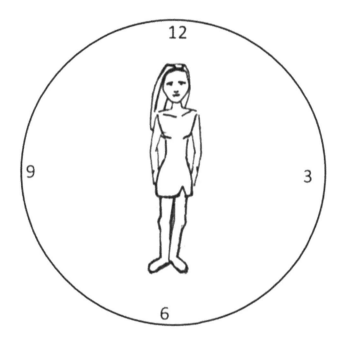

3: Buckets:

Buckets

Buckets are in the fist position with fingers facing the floor, as if you were grasping a bucket handle. This would be in "T", broken T's, and even low V's.

4: Candlesticks/Table Tops:

Hand position in fists, straight in front of you from the shoulder for candlesticks, or elbows bent at waist and fists close to your chest for a Table Tops.

Candlesticks

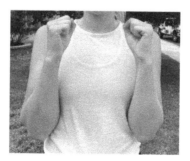

Table Top

5: Clean:

Standing straight, feet together, arms straight down at your sides. Can be done with blades or fists depending on preference and reason for use.

6: **Fists or Thumbs/Pinkies:**
Hand is closed, thumb curled over the outside of the fingers.

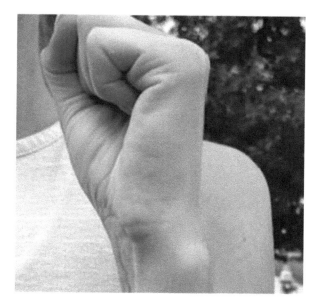

Fists Inside / Pinkies

Fists Outside / Thumbs

7: Floor Clock:

The Floor Clock is my way of explaining where to turn or where other things are in relation to your body. Think of yourself as standing at the center of a clock painted around you on the floor, with the judges (or your audience) sitting at 6:00, and 12:00 being directly behind you. Front Hurdlers will face at 4-4:30 or 7:30-8, left and right respectively on the floor clock. When you turn completely sideways to the judges you will be at 3:00 or 9:00 on the floor clock, as in a Pike Jump.

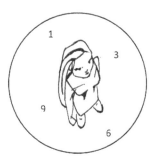

8: Ready Position:

Standing straight, feet together or at shoulder width, as determined by your coach or the activity, fists on hips. (Never use a "taco" hand to hold the hip. That is a dance move, not cheer).

9: Tacos:

Hand is in a "V", with fingers straight and thumb held at an angle to form the "V". Might be used in a cheer dance but should not be used in ready position.

Tacos Hands

10: Body Printing:

The process of imprinting the correct position on your muscles before doing a jump or executing a dance move. If you don't know how your body should feel in the correct position, it's difficult to achieve it while in motion. See Chapter 7 for Body Printing.

11: By 8 Count:

The 8 count is the standard measure for cheers, chants or dances. All will be broken into sections of 8 counts. Even jumps are counts as 8 steps from prep to landing.

12: Crab Step:

This is my name for the sideways "skip" that you use in your entrance with spiriting. It is done by stepping to the side in long, bouncy strides. Step out with your lead foot, then bring the second foot to it – almost a sideways galloping step. This will allow you to keep facing the judges as you spirit in. Later, you will use this at games and other events to enter and move to position in the cheer space without turning your back to the crowd.

13: Flat foot:

Keeping your feet flat on the ground in a jump prep. This is sometimes required by coaches during jump preps. If it's not required, do not do it. Prep on the toe provides more power and allows you to use your arm momentum more effectively. If flat footing jumps is required, you can partially recreate the extra lift advantage of a prep at the toe by squeezing the muscles of your feet and legs during the prep.

14: Groundwork:

Any movement or sequence that requires the participant to put anything other than their feet on the ground. Seat Rolls, going to knees and back up (without looking awkward or getting hurt – NO KNEE DROPS!) or even lying flat are examples of groundwork.

15: Pop Out:

Usually at the end of spiriting or a cheer or dance. Snap into a High V, feet apart position. It must be crisp and sharp. Not a sweep. Very effective from slightly bent legs and tabletops straight out the High V & feet apart.

16: Prep:

Prep is the position from which you launch your jump. Each jump has an expected prep, either because the action helps with the execution of the jump, or as decided by a specific coach or group (school district, camp company, gym, competition host company, etc....) This is where your momentum for the jump comes from. By allowing your body to stretch up with arms extended, then bending your knees and using the force of your arms swinging from prep to jump position, you can gain greater height and power in your jumps. You will learn more in Chapter 8 Jumps Step by Step

17: Pull:

Any motion in which you appear to pull your arms from an extended motion back towards your core forcefully. It can also be a spiriting or cheer motion where you step forward with one foot, pretend to grasp a bar with both hands at buckets, then appear to pull yourself forward, dragging the back foot up and snapping it into place beside the other.

18: Punch It:

Punching it is putting emphasis on a motion but not necessarily with a fist. It simply means to give a sharp, defined feel to a motion or movement.

19: Spiriting:

Yes, it is a noun! Spiriting is the collection of motions and phrases you use to fire up your crowd, or in the case of tryouts, the judges. Spiriting is done on entrance, after each jump, chant, cheer, and dance during your tryout, unless you are specifically instructed not to. Your spiriting helps the judges identify with you as a cheer-leader and lets them see that you have the skill and enthusiasm to engage a crowd. Spiriting at tryouts, when there is no team to encourage, also lets the judges see that you can still create excite-ment with your attitude, actions, and voice at the time when your team and crowd may need it most – the inevitable down times in a game. Tryouts are all about making the judges see you as a cheer-leader before you are one!

20: Stunting:

Stunts are anything that requires more than one person and in-volves at least one person supporting another off the ground. Examples range from a thigh stand to any type of large group pyra-mids. We will not discuss that here as tryouts seldom involve stunting.

21: Sweep:

Up or out- up as from low touchdown or V to high touchdown or V, half or full – it is a cheer, dance, or spirting move. Usually in a more rounded motion as opposed to straight and sharp.

22: Who Can You Beat:

This is an exercise by which you analyze the skills of those you will compete against for a spot in the squad. Ignore seniors – they are gone. You can do this at games during the year and before tryouts, and especially during tryouts week. DO NOT try to video them or be obvious about noting their skills. Just pay attention. Look at jumps, motions, overall floor presence. Are you better? Can you be? Remember you only need one spot. We will discuss this in more in the Chapter 10: Dance Learn to Learn sections.

23: **X:**

X in a written cheer means "clap"

Now let's look at types of cheer and where you fit in.

CHAPTER 3

Sideline vs Competitive What's Right for you?

Sideline cheer does not significantly help you do competitive cheer, unless exposure to it makes you want to try competitive. While they share some skills like jumps, motions, and the need to smile constantly, they are very different in the use of those skills. Sideline is designed to support a sports team and excite the crowd to support them as well. Competitive cheer is designed to win competitions. Crowd excitement is in support of the cheerleaders themselves. It is therefore geared to the purpose of appealing to judges first, and crowds second, by marking points within a routine set to music.

Involvement in competitive cheer may strengthen your base skills, but it will not teach you to sideline cheer. In fact, there are some competitive habits that must be unlearned to succeed at tryouts for a school squad. For instance, "pouty" or over-emphasized facials, and heavy makeup are common and encouraged in competitive cheer. They are also a sure way to lose points at school tryouts.

Jumps that are bad in form but still high are sometimes buried in the crowd on a competition team because having no feet hanging in view of the judges is sufficient to gain points. At school tryouts, you will do your jumps alone on the floor and be judged on your height, form, landing, and whether you maintain a smile from beginning to end! Big difference in the need to train form in jumps.

Tumbling rules the day in competitive cheer. Skill level, more than age, is the main criteria for moving up to the next team at most gyms. In school cheer, there is usually a district limit on tumbling as to the level of difficulty allowed, generally limited to tucks or below in public high school, with often no tumbling in junior high tryouts at all.

Representing your school is part of making your school squad. The notoriety of belonging to a competitive gym is in the camaraderie found there, and in the distinction of being part of a gym that wins, if it does. Do not expect your competition team to win you friends or rec-ognition at school, unless you go to school with other team members. You can expect making a school squad to win you at least recognition, if not popularity in your school.

Again - what's your **WHY**? And where does it fit best?

Consider the obvious differences first. A competition team can have many participants, but typically includes at least a few that have weaker skills. A competitive cheer gym has many teams and so will find room for almost anyone, placing them on a team that suits their age and skill level. Tryouts are held annually and are based entirely on skill. A team member is assured of being placed where they will have the best im-pact. The teams will continue to be teaching grounds to improve skills, overcome fears, and develop a floor presence. Competitive coaches have a vested interest in helping team members succeed in improving their skills.

A school cheer squad has a limited number of participants, as dic-tated by either the school or sport conference. Only a certain number of cheerleaders are allowed on the field or floor at any given time, and sometimes only in a certain space. Tryouts are held annually, and they are based not only on skill, but also floor presence, personality, appearance, and frankly, volume! Although most squads consist of members with similar skills, it is possible for someone with significantly less skill to make a squad in order to fill the allotted number of participants. While tryouts scores are held in confidence, it is often painfully obvious who came in last. This can be difficult emotionally for low performers on an 8-to-12-person squad where the difference shows with every performance. Unfortunately, helping that person improve is not expected, and in many cases not even possible on a school squad. An inexperienced teacher may be the faculty advisor, as opposed to a qualified coach. However well intentioned, they may not be equipped to train skills and the child is either left at the bottom, or lessons at a gym become necessary.

It is harder to make your school squad than to join a local competition cheer gym. But is it right for you?

Cons for Competitive Cheer:

No way around it, competitive cheer is expensive. You are required to pay tuition, uniform, training, competition fees, as well as make up, practice gear and shoes. This can hit any price range, and there may be extra purchases required along the way. Also, travel to competitions is mandatory and extra, as are entrance tickets for family members, as well as food and lodging for all. Typically, a parent or guardian is required to attend each competition with their cheerleader for reasons of liability. This can quickly add up to more than the average family can afford, and once the commitment is made, your contract may require a buyout price to quit. That said, it can still be a great way to deal with lack of experience before school tryouts.

Some points to remember:

1. You will be required to wear the uniform, hair style and make-up the gym chooses, regardless of comfort level with short skirts, bared midriffs, or heavy make-up on young girls. Likewise, practice uniforms will often be briefs and sports bras as opposed to t-shirts and gym shorts. Again, your family's comfort level must be considered before signing up.

2. Your competition gym isn't school, and you won't be allowed to wear the uniform in class.

3. Tumbling training will likely be better if you are on a team at the gym. They incorporate training into practice time, working skill levels into routines and teaching new skills as needed. Regular tumbling class is usually required and may or may not be included in the cost. The instructors are the same instructors who will teach you if you don't join a team, but you will not receive extra class or practice time. Most gyms offer "open gym" time where you might get extra help, but more often you would need to schedule extra paid private lessons with your instructor for individual help.

4. Private lessons with a competitive coach can be scheduled for help with school tryouts skills, but keep in mind that they will not continue to make money after you make the squad. Offers to join the competitive team instead, and repeated reassurance that "you can always cheer here" should be discouraged. It should be made clear at the first lesson that you are not interested in joining their gym. The simple reason is if you begin to rely on the idea that you don't have to make school cheer, you probably won't work hard enough for it to happen. Most competitive coaches are ethical enough to properly train you to succeed at school tryouts since they will gain a more positive reputation if you do. However, have your parents fully research the gym to determine their financial stability and whether they would benefit more from your success or failure outside of their business model.

Likewise, due diligence should be done to determine if your school squad is run in a safe and ethical manner. Complaints or history of injuries would be easily available.

Cons for School Cheer:

Sideline Cheer is academically ruled. If you struggle with your grades, you may find that you work for months learning skills, pay good money for tumbling lessons, make the squad, and then don't get to cheer because you don't remain academically eligible. Competitive cheer will not consider your grades. That will be up to your parents. School will qualify you by grading period, monthly, or even weekly. You must perform academically to participate in school cheer.

Sideline Cheer is time consuming. So is competitive, but the practices and competitions are scheduled ahead, and you will have a general idea of when extra practices will be called. You will know travel day expectancy as well. School can throw you curve balls. You may be asked to attend events at the school, such as orientations, fish camps, or family nights, that you weren't expecting. You may be required to perform at a store grand opening or for a last-minute town pep rally if your team makes it to playoffs, or state. "Sorry, I have plans" is not an option. You will need to be committed and flexible.

Sideline Cheer has rules that extend outside of school. On or off campus, you will be a representative of your squad and school. People in town may know you. You must be polite and kind in public, and certainly you will not be allowed to participate in PDA, drinking alcohol or smoking while you are a squad member. Even posting on social media may be regulated by content. Be sure you want to "walk the line" before you go to the trouble of earning the spot.

School cheer is very visible and while the popularity may seem fun, the lack of privacy can be overwhelming if you aren't used to it. The days of walking the halls unnoticed are over. Bad hair days and outfit disasters will be noticed. If you are self-confident and secure, it's not a problem. It's even fun to be noticed. If you like to be anonymous some days, this aspect of cheer may be difficult.

Since we're on the subject of clothes and appearance, let's look at your clinic and tryouts "look", and the reasons why it matters!

CHAPTER 4

Dress for Success

Here are some items you need! You don't have to spend a fortune - hundreds of dollars on shoes isn't required. You need cheer shoes, and good ones, but you must find out what you will be required to wear for tryouts first. Go and talk to the cheer coach for whom you will be trying out. Some schools have restrictions on the shoes that can be worn, and most all require a certain type of outfit, in certain colors.

The usual restrictions include:

1. No squad shoes that will indicate you cheered on last year's squad -colored inserts or monogrammed, etc.... this provides judges with a clear indication of returning cheerleaders and is considered an unfair advantage in good programs.

2. No squad bows that specifically indicate a returning cheerleader. (See above)

3. Spaghetti strap tank tops, tube tops, or anything see through. (The judges just don't want to know you that well!)

4. No super short shorts. (Same reason...)

My recommendations:

Shoes:

For tryouts you need to focus on a good shoe, not too costly, with as light a weight you can find without sacrificing support, AND one that you can tumble in. The weight of a shoe may not sound important, but it matters. Try to stay at 11 oz or less. That said, in the beginning, you don't need extra weight while you're learning the basics and getting your height. Once you've achieved good height and form, you may want to add light, strap-on ankle weights. At that point (and NOT before) the extra weight will give you the benefit of continuing to build muscle. When you take them off for tryouts, your legs will fly from the habit of lifting more weight. $30-$90 are good prices for shoes. If you can find closeouts cheaper, that's great but read the reviews and customer remarks carefully. Hint - do not put non-prescription shoes inserts in. They can cause your foot to shift and injure you. Also, the gel type may burst on impact from jumps!

Do not buy them big!

Adults paying the bill: I know this is tough because "room to grow" is a real thing, but they must fit or you risk injuring your child, which is much more expensive in the long run. And they must be updated for size regularly.

The shoe must be tied tightly – not to cut off circulation, but so much that it stays secure to your foot. Start at the bottom of the laces and pull them tight as you work your way up to the tie (tie a bow, then tie the two loops and strings again to secure). You will notice a difference in the stability of your jumps and dance immediately and never complain about it again. I promise... Go for all white, and they must be immaculate for tryouts. If you need to buy two pairs, so be it, but you can keep them clean if you try. Also – the second pair must be broken in at least a month before tryouts. New shoes are very difficult to perform in.

Tryouts clothes:
No basketball or long shorts. Not super short shorts, but they need to be short enough to keep you from looking clumsy and dowdy. You don't want your bottom hanging out, but you will look clunky in shorts that are too long.

Your best bet is to look online for cheer shorts. You will see inexpensive knit shorts in several brands, in every color. One brand will stand out - buy something like those. And don't buy them big or small. They need to fit, and not droop or fit like shrink wrap. Get your real size, not the size you wish you were. And don't roll the waistband down. Judges don't typically like that. It hitches the crotch up tight, and again - they don't want to know you that well!

Get appropriate cheer shorts in the color specified by tryouts rules. If they don't specify, buy brand new **black** ones for tryouts day. Never wear the black shorts you have on hand. After a few washings, knit shorts look faded. New, crisp cheer shorts are around $10 - $20 if not on sale. Make the investment every year. Even if you can't tell, when three girls line up together in tryouts, the judges can see who looks worn out. Shorts are not to be confused with briefs or "spanks".

You need shorts to wear but you also need briefs or spanks for UNDER the shorts. If you've never worn them, it's a different feeling and therefore you need to wear them to practice. They serve several purposes. First, they preserve your dignity by hugging your body and maintaining coverage in the crotch. Second, they are made of slick material that allows your shorts to drop back into place after your tricks, not bunch up. Third, they hide sweat. There's nothing less attractive than bright colored, knit shorts with a big "V" sweat stain in front or back. The black is also good for this problem. Match the color of your spanks to your tryout's shorts. For practice, you can mix, but for tryouts always match.

Shirts are more subjective. You need to look at your body type. V necks, round necks, scoop necks (NOT deep and plunging) are popular, and can be paired with traditional short sleeves, or cap sleeves. DO NOT choose long sleeves, 3/4 sleeves, sleeveless at the shoulder, or tanks/camisoles, unless specified by the coach. If not specified, choose a white knit that isn't too tight or too sheer. Try every type and look at yourself doing cheer motions in the changing room. Does it ride up and show belly? Nope. Bunches on the shoulder? Nope. In which sleeve/neckline combo do your arms and shoulders look best at Clean position? Don't buy what you like to wear - buy what looks right on you. Look at your bust line and waistline critically to choose the top that best suits your body shape. It doesn't matter your size if you are strong, can do the tricks, and you present yourself in clothes that fit and look neat. And ALWAYS WEAR A SPORTS BRA THAT FITS TIGHT ENOUGH TO PROVIDE SUPPORT AND MINIMIZE MOVEMENT, IN THE SAME COLOR AS YOUR SHIRT. Besides being unattractive, "bounce" is bad for your back and can result in pain, stretch marks, and sagging tissue over time, not to mention it throws your center of balance off, affecting your performance.

Jewelry:
Fingers, toes, ears, necks, wrists, ankles, belly buttons, lips, noses, and anything else that could be pierced or adorned should be jewelry free, even if the rules don't state it. Wearing a purity or engagement ring? Don't wear it. You won't be put in a position to need that distinction on the cheer floor. Besides, rings are not allowed when cheering for safety reasons, and the judges will notice if you ignore that cardinal rule at tryouts.

Hair and Makeup:
As a rule, tryouts hair and makeup should be neat and minimal. Make-up is necessary but in moderation. Some coaches expect red lipstick, others don't. This should be in the tryout's requirements. DO NOT indulge in heavy street make-up, or in any kind of competitive make up, glitter or costumed eye shadows. Traditionally, you want to be reasonably natural, but with even skin tone. If that requires a light base or powder, do it. But be very careful, as you don't want makeup marks on your shirt when you hit the tryouts floor. Eyes should be natural, with only mascara.

Go with waterproof - no explanation needed. Stick with black, or dark brown, as complements your skin tone. No colors. No colored eyeshadow or lipsticks unless red or pink lips are required. This isn't to be boring - it's to keep from distracting the judge's eye from your skills. If they are looking at your bright make up, they aren't looking at your awesome skills.

The same goes for your nails -

Nails:
Should be of a reasonably short length. Due to safety in stunting and tumbling, most squads do not allow long nails. Remove color and go with a natural, clear polish. If your nails are discolored from previous nail polish or enhancements, a pale, natural looking pink will cover it without standing out. Colored nails will draw attention away from

your motions, or worse, they highlight poor placement or any motion errors. This is why most squads do not allow colored nails during games or performances. Watch a video and you'll know exactly who was off based on the flash of bright colored fingertips where they shouldn't be, at the wrong time.

Hair:

Should be in your natural color, or at least in a color that grows naturally from a human head. This is not a time for fun dye colors, either all over or on the tips. Even the school colors would not win you points in cheer tryouts, so your whole head in neon pink will likely only distract the judges' eye, lowering your overall score.

Likewise, longer hair should be pulled up neatly into as high a ponytail as compliments your face. The best set is at the back end of your part, angled slightly back. A ponytail set on top, in the center of your head looks awkward and is impractical. Same for a low ponytail at the back of your neck. The top-of-your-head pony will flop to the side or front, falling into your eyes and distracting the judges. The low pony at the base of the neck will slip out, or bunch up when your shoulders move, restricting your motion. It will also leave you looking plain from the front as your bow won't show.

If you have short hair, go for half up, half down, and if you must put the pony high on the head, place your bow on top of the elastic and clip it down, to flatten the height of the pony. You should always wear a bow unless restricted by the rules.

Hair too short for a pony at all? Clip the bow to the top of your hair, at the back of the part. Consult a hairdresser on the best method to keep it in your hair, but pin curls, gel and hair spray will likely be involved. Hair so short that no bow is possible may consider leaving it off. If so, you must compensate by being as expressive as possible to bring the judges' eyes back to your face, which is the true purpose of a bow at tryouts. Just don't resort to making faces or blowing kisses. That's not a school thing.

Bow:

Again, the purpose of bows at tryouts is to draw the judge's eye to your face. Go for a large enough bow to show up well, but not so large as to flop, pull down the ponytail, or be so heavy that it falls out. Most often, the rules will state that you cannot use the cheer bows from last season, again to discourage unfair advantage. A solid white (dark or medium brown hair) or black (Light brown to blonde hair) is almost always your best bet if your school color is either not allowed, or if it doesn't suit your coloring. (Exp: An orange bow on bright red hair is a mistake even if it's your school color. Go for the alternate color or default to black or white - whichever compliments you). If you are required to wear an uncomplimentary color, then you need to get creative. Try a bow with a thin layer of white or black along the edge to keep the wrong color off of your hair. Don't use glitter, sequins, spiral corkscrews, or anything that bobs or flashes. You can use a striped bow (a white, black, school color combo is usually acceptable if not too busy) Your bow should be at least a two-inch-wide ribbon and should not look like the bow is wearing your head, instead of the other way around! A huge "bat wing" bow is - again - distracting! You want to stand out and be memorable, but you do that with bright eyes (in a moderate amount of dark tone mascara), a bright, happy smile, and great skills! NOT by being under-dressed, over painted, and wearing something on your head that looks as if it might take flight and carry you away!

CHAPTER 5

Motions

Cheer motions are, for the most part, a common set of arm and leg placements that are somewhat standard across the industry. Your local area may have a different name for them, but usually they are referred to in some way like the below listed explanations. The internet is filled with pictures and drawings of motions. Any that are published by the big cheer training companies will be safe to use.

**First and foremost, never have loose, sloppy, drooping arms, commonly called "spaghetti arms". Always hold your whole body tight, muscles ready to move, looking sharp and at attention.

Never "cock" your wrists. Always keep them straight and rotate your fist slightly back, as pictured.

Cocked Wrists Down   **Cocked Wrists Up**

Aside from Ready Positions, either blades or fists can be used in most motions, as preferred, or indicated in the cheer or routine. Blades are used in the explanations. Fists would face the same direction as blades.

1: **Ready position:**

Floor Clock
(Facing 6:00)

Body Clock
(Elbows 3:00 & 9:00)

For Fists on hips, standing straight with feet together, or at shoulder width (**Ready At Shoulder**). Be sure your shoulders are rolled forward, and elbows are straight. Never let them drift back — that looks like wings from the front. It's weak and looks sloppy.

2: Touchdown:

Floor Clock
(Facing 6:00)

Body Clock
(Hands 12:00)

Arms extended above head, straight up at the shoulder, hands in blades, palms facing each other. Extend slightly forward towards your crowd.

3: Low Touchdown:

Floor Clock
(Facing 6:00)

Body Clock
(Hands 6:00)

Arms extended straight down, resting just inside the shoulder line, at candlesticks. Push your shoulders slightly forward allowing your arms to maintain a straight line, resting a few inches in front of the outer third of thighs.

4: High "V":

Floor Clock
(Feet @ 6:00)

Body Clock
(Hands 11:00 & 1:00)

Arms extended above head, hands in blades, at Thumbs, palms facing away from each other.

5: Half High "V":

Floor Clock
(Feet @ 6:00)

Body Clock
(Hands 11:00 or 2:00)

Right or left arm in high "V", the other fist on hip. Right or left high "V" is determined by which arm is raised. Your right or left, not the audience's.

6: Low "V":

Floor Clock
(Fists @ 4:00 & 8:00)

Body Clock
(Hands 4:30 & 7:30)

Arms extended down, at 4:00 and 8:00, hands in blades, at thumbs, palms facing down.

7: Half Low "V":

Floor Clock
(Fists @ 4:00 & 8:00)

Body Clock
(Hands 4:30 or 7:30)

As with the half high "V", the half low uses one arm extended to low "V" and the other fist on hip.

8: "T":

Floor Clock
(Fists @ (8:30 & 3:30)

Body Clock
(Hands 3:00 & 9:00)

Arms straight out to the sides, shoulder height, in blades or fists. Fists are in buckets.

9: Broken T:

Floor Clock
(Elbows @ 3:00 & 9:00)

Body Clock
(Elbows 3:00 & 9:00)

Arms at shoulder height, elbows pointing straight out to the sides, forearms bent back into the middle of the chest, hands presenting in Table Tops, buckets, or blades.

10: Half T:

Floor Clock
(Arms @ 3:00 & 9:00)

Body Clock
(Elbow 3:00 or 9:00)

One arm is in T position, the other is in Half T position. Right or left is determined by the straight arm. Hands may be buckets or blades.

11: Candlesticks:

Floor Clock
(Hands @ 6:00)

Body Clock
(Hands forward 3:00 & 9:00)

Arms are extended in front of you, shoulder height. Hands are in Candlesticks, Thumbs facing up, fingers facing toward each other.

12: Table Tops:

Floor Clock
(Hands @ 6:00)

Body Clock
(Hands @ 3:00 & 9:00)

As a motion, Table Tops are done with elbows bent, arms hugged in and touching your sides. Hands will be in fists, just inside your shoulder line, pinkies facing out. Your upper arms will press in against your chest and shoulders should be tensed and strong, slightly forward.

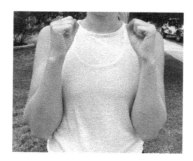

13: Hands:

Blades or fists your hand position is important. Fists are NEVER used with fingers facing the crowd. Always rotate your fist so that the side of your hand faces in or out. Likewise, the blade will be side facing. The only exceptions would be a "stop"; motion with the hand cocked up and the palm facing the crowd during a cheer or routine.

A. Fists always face the crowd with the side of your hand. The side where your thumb and index finger meet will be called outside fists. The side where your little finger presents will be called inside fists. In youth leagues, this is sometimes described as Big O vs Little O.

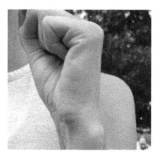

B. Blades always present the side of the hand to the crowd, either facing up or down. We will refer to them as thumbs or pinkies, depending on which side is presented to the crowd. Very occasionally you will see blades at Broken "T", facing the chest. This is most likely only during a dance routine and palms, in my opinion, an awkward looking placement. Don't use it for tryouts unless it is required.

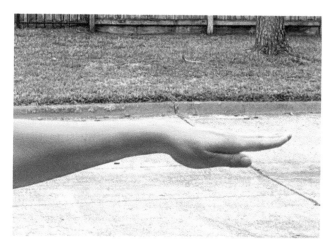

14. Bucket Drill:

A good way to determine proper hand placement is to run through the arm motions in order and think of yourself as holding a bucket full of water in each hand. The bucket handle does not swivel so it will always hang from your hand in the same direction. Start at Low Touchdown and decide could you comfortably hold a bucket of water with your hands in thumbs? Yes. In Pinkies? To present pinkies at that position, you would need to rotate your hands around so that the top of your hands your thumbs are against your thighs, fingers facing away from each other. Not comfortable and obviously not the correct position. So, thumbs at Low Touchdown. Move on to Low V. Do you feel more comfortable with your fist fingers facing up or down? Down, therefore still presenting thumbs. Move to T - again thumbs down will be the correct position to hold a bucket. High V? Still thumbs down (just because). Touchdown? Finally, you are at Pinkies in the air. Picture the full bucket hanging down against your arm. Would you have the strength to hold it if you rotated your hands away from each other? Could you even do that? Maybe you can if you are double jointed, and if you are…don't. :D

Now that you have the motions, let's move to the most important skill in school cheer. Jumps!

CHAPTER 6

Jumps - What are They?

Cheerleading jumps are skills in which the body is moved into specific positions in the air. To perform jumps properly, the athlete must jump high enough and stay up long enough to assume the required position, then still land lightly, with feet together.

There are 5 basic jumps. Some programs use them all. Some only 3. They are: Right Front Hurdler, Left Front Hurdler, Right Side Hurdler, Left Side Hurdler, and Toe Touch. Chapter 8: Jumps Step by Step will explain each of these individually.

There are other jumps not commonly used for tryouts – or at least they shouldn't be. One is the Pike Jump. The Pike is very difficult to do correctly and takes a great deal of flexibility and height. While it may seem that doing the 'hard' jump even marginally well would get you more points, don't fool yourself. A poorly done Pike Jump will get you less points than doing a less than perfect common jump. There is no 'A for effort' in tryouts. Unless it's absolutely perfect, don't do it. (Don't let someone you're competing with tell you it's perfect and you should definitely do it. Note the phrase 'competing with'. They do not have your best interests at heart.)

The other commonly known jump is the Herkie. In a Herkie, the front leg extends forward from the hip, body faces 5:00/7:00 on the floor, and the back leg is bent with the knee pointing toward the ground and the foot pointed up in the back. Due to the slight angle of the body, the foot will be clearly visible from the front. The straight leg side will be hand on hip and the bent leg side will be a half high touchdown in fist.

While the Herkie is like a Side Hurdler, the difference is in the back (or bent) leg. In the Side Hurdler, like in a Hurdler Stretch, the back leg is bent, level with the hip. The lower leg and foot are pushed behind your body and should not drift down into clear sight. **Some stretch the back leg out and allow the foot to be more visible. As long as the knee remains bent and level with the hip, this should not change the score. However, if the back leg is too straight, there is danger of this being seen as a badly done split jump (a dancer's move) and points would be lost. It is safer to tuck the foot away behind you, and frankly, it's easier.

The Side Hurdler is often referred to as a Herkie in junior high and high schools. To do a Herkie in the correct form (knee bent towards the ground) for tryouts will likely result in a lower score than a true Side Hurdler. Consult the program's coach for verification of which jump they require and what they call it. (I don't recommend pointing it out if they have it wrong…)

You can also watch the current cheerleaders at your school and get an idea of which jump is used. This is where "Who Can You Beat" begins. Start setting your baselines and get to know your competition.

"Who Can You Beat" is the process of watching others who either are cheering or who intend to tryout and sizing up your competition. Be honest. If you aren't sure that you can score better than someone else, make their skills your motivation to improve. When tryouts arrive, if you have been honest, you will know that you have the skills to win one of the spots on the squad just by knowing "Who Can You Beat?"

Body Clock   **Floor Clock**

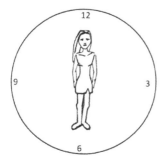   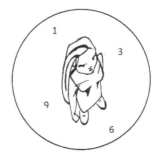

1. **V Prep for Front Facing Jumps:**

   Floor Clock　　**Body Clock**
   (Feet @ 6:00)　　(Hands 11:00 & 1:00)

   Start at Ready Position, facing your audience. Clean. In a fluid motion, bring your arms from clean to clasp, keeping your elbows against your ribcage. This will be slightly different for each person. Let your hands meet in front of your chest, legs slightly bent. Immediately push up to high "V", going to toes. Crest and pull each arm down in two large circles, crossing in front of your torso, using shoulders, not just arms. From the hip, pull straight back up, lifting to the sides, stopping sharp at "T".

2. **Prep for Side Facing Jumps:**

Body Clock
(Hands 11:00 & 1:00)

Floor Clock
(Front Hurdlers face 6:00/4:00-4:30/6:00
or 6:00/7:30-8:00/6:00)

Start at Ready Position, facing your audience. Clean. In a fluid motion, turn to prep, right or left. As you turn, bring your arms from clean to hands clasped around the top of your rib-cage. This will be slightly different for each person. Keep your elbows against your sides, and let your hands meet in front of you, legs slightly crouched. Immediately push up to the high "V", going to toes. Crest and pull down, using shoulders, not just arms. From the hip, pull straight back up, lifting to the sides not straight up in front of you.

3. **Rocket Prep**

   Floor Clock
   (Feet @ 6:00, turning to 4:30 or 7:30)

   Body Clock
   (Hands 10:00 & 2:00)

It is so named because the arm placement is like a rocket taking off from your chest. Proper arm placement, with shoulder muscles engaged, will have your upper arms at your cheeks. *Too far back and your face will be pushed between your arms. Too far forward and your shoulders will strain and start to hyperextend. Either way, you will feel the power decrease in your shoulders and back. *

Rocket Prep

Start at Ready Position, facing your audience. Clean. In a fluid motion, turn to the correct direction for your jump, bring your arms from clean to clasp at the chest. This will be slightly different for each person. Keep your elbows against your sides, and let your hands meet in front of you, legs slightly bent. Immediately push up to the rocket position, going to toes. Crest and pull down in front of you, using shoulders, not just arms. Do not unclasp your hands until you reach waist or hip level in front of you - your body will determine when to let go at the natural spot based on your arms and your build. Just keep your arms straight and let go before you hit your thighs. From the hip, pull back up to the top again, lifting slightly to the sides rather than straight up in front of you.

3. **Landing for front or side facing jumps:**

   Floor Clock
   (Feet @ 6:00)

   Returning to the ground, your arms should snap back down to your sides, and you will push your chest up to keep your back straighter. This also helps your body to stay aloft longer as you jump back down. Land in a slight crouch (to save your knees) with arms in clean. Then snap back to the ready position, rotating to the front if you are side facing.

   Tip:

   Allow your chin to drop a little when you land and snap it up to meet the judges' eyes when you return to ready position. If not, you run the risk of the judges staring straight up your nose instead of meeting your eyes as you come out of a jump.

CHAPTER 7

Before You Jump

Repetition rules! Start with 5 of each jump, or 25 total per day. If you have never jumped before you can start with 3 but push yourself to 5 within the first week. The next week do 7 to 10 of each jump. Move up every week without fail – even if it's only by one more jump! Progress matters. Work your way up to doing 100 jumps a day, in one session, with only short stops for rest in between groups of jumps. That's 20 of each jump – Toe Touch, Right and Left Side Hurdlers, and Right and Left Front Hurdlers. You will be sore. It will be uncomfortable.

But nothing worth having is easy, right?

Don't think you can do it? Tell yourself you can.

What your mouth says, your ears hear, your mind believes.

Flexibility is equally as important as strength and endurance. You can jump all day, and if your leg muscles are not stretched enough, you will never achieve the jumps that will win you a place on the squad. And you might just hurt yourself in the process.

Stretching is *Critical*

Do not bounce when you stretch!! That's a quick way to a pulled muscle. Lean over and stretch gently, letting your muscles get accustomed to the position. As days and weeks go by you will stretch further and further until you reach your goal of head to knee or floor and chest laid flat, not arched!

Stay in each stretch for as long as you can at first, and then begin to set times as your flexibility increases - You can stretch in front of the tv, or while you read. (Stretch through the show and jump during the commercials! This will also keep your family off your back if you're in your home's common area).

1. **Straddle Stretch:**
   Don't worry if you can't touch your nose to your knee, much less to the ground in the center! Everyone starts somewhere. Sit down, spread your legs apart as far as you can, legs straight, knees facing the ceiling. Straighten your back and lean forward into the middle, hands reaching out to both feet. Change and lean over one leg, reaching to the one foot, then the other.

Straddle Side Stretch

2. **Hurdler Stretch:**

   Same goes here. Don't worry if you're not down to your knee on either side. You will be. Sit in the hurdler position, one leg straight, one leg bent with the foot tucked behind you. Keep your straight knee pointed up at the ceiling, **not** rolled to point at the wall behind you. Push your back/bent leg as far behind you as you can, and lean down over the other leg, hands reaching to the foot. Rest your nose on your knee, and eventually pass your knee to the floor. Change sides and stretch over the other leg.

   Hurdler Stretch

3. **Butterfly Stretch:**

   Sit straight, feet together in front of you, knees out to each side. Grasp your feet and use your elbows to push down gently. Don't hunch over — it's hard on your lower back if you do. Eventually your legs will press easily to the ground in this position.

   Butterfly Stretch

4. **Wall Stretch:**

This is more effective than you may think! Lay on the floor (carpet or a blanket is recommended as you'll be here for a while!) and scoot up against the wall, placing the backs of your legs against the wall, feet above you.

Wall Stretch

(Just wear socks so as not to mess up the wall!) Make sure your bottom is completely against the wall, then let your feet slide down on either side, keeping your legs straight. You will be in a Straddle Stretch position with your legs above you, to each side. Now, let gravity do its thing. Get comfortable and listen to music, look at your phone, watch a movie (you can turn your head, but don't raise it.) Better yet, read a book! This will also strengthen your arms because you need to hold it above you! Hold it at arms-length, with both hands. Don't stay TOO long though! You could experience some tingling (foot goes "to sleep") and perhaps stiffness when you get up the first few times. Use good sense and get up if you begin to have tingling or pain.

5. **Couch Stretch:**

    This is a safer alternative to the popular double stretch that so many teams and gyms use. In a double stretch, two people sit facing in a straddle stretch. They grasp hands, one person puts their feet on the other's ankles or lower calves, and they lay back, pulling the other person down into a straddle stretch. There are a couple of problems with this. First, you can only do it with a partner! Second, you can't control the level of stretch your partner gives you, or how fast. If they decide to yank on your hands, you can pull a muscle. It's not funny, even if they "didn't mean to." Remember, this is tryouts. And everyone isn't your friend. Even if they're sorry, you're still not jumping for days, maybe weeks... which will set you way behind on practicing and could stop you from trying out at all.

    Try this instead:

    Sit in front of your couch, straddle stretch position with your feet against the bottom of the couch (not under it). Grasp the bottom edge of the couch and pull forward as far as you're comfortable, then a little more. You want to feel it, but not hurt yourself. Be wise - slow and steady rules the day. When you're as far as you can go, rest your hands, arms, or head (depending on how close you are) on the couch and relax. Read a book, do homework, watch a movie – talk to your parents! Believe me, they will probably be excited if you ask them to keep you company! Sit in this position for as long as you're comfortable. Again, be reasonable. Pain, tingling, etc. are signs your legs have had enough. Time to get up.

Couch Stretch

6. **Chair Lift:**

   Chair lifts are a great exercise for jump strength. Stand by a chair, steady yourself by holding the back, and lift your leg to the side, knee straight, foot and knee rotated towards the ceiling, toe pointed, leg slightly forward from your hip. From a dead lift, it's not as easy as it sounds. That's your first clue to how strong your leg muscles are. Now close your eyes and identify which muscles are in use to lift your leg. Squeeze that muscle hard and feel what it's like to lift that leg into the proper position. Look at your leg, and where it is in relation to your hip. (Notice that we haven't put it down yet... no, you can't rest it on the arm of the chair. There's that strength thing again!) Now, reverse directions and snap that leg back down next to the one still on the ground. Snap it down hard, don't just let it fall back in exhaustion. Lift back up and do it again, focusing on which muscles you used to snap it back down.

BODY PRINTING

Body Printing is the process of conditioning your body and muscles to feel a jump. If you've never done a jump correctly, how can you expect your body to recreate what you see immediately, without any help in discovering where it needs to go? Body Printing involves putting yourself into the position on the ground and imprinting how it feels on your mind. While in the position, close your eyes and squeeze all your muscles as hard as you can to the count of ten. Feel your body – feel where your leg comes out of your hip socket, how it feels in the right position. Feel your back knee and ankle and mentally note the degree of twist needed to move your back leg into that position. Feel your back, shoulders, neck, arms, hands. Repeat it several times until you've focused on every part of your body in that position. Do this exercise every time you start to do jumps. Even stop between jumps and use it to reset your body to the correct position. Soon you'll be hitting it in the air without trouble.

The proper body print for a toe touch is a straddle stretch. Keep your back straight, arms outstretched over your legs, arms in "T" hands in buckets. The proper ground position for a Front Hurdler is a Hurdler Stretch, adjusting so that your fists are in position beside your front foot and your face and eyes are turned upwards towards them, while your chest is parallel to your front leg.

Straddle Stretch

Can't do a full straddle split? So what! Not many can! Just move your legs out as far as you possibly can, stay in position, and keep your head up, smiling as if you are jumping for the judges. Do this in front of your mirror image. From the front, even legs that aren't in full straddle splits look like a good toe touch. The more you stretch and practice, the further out your legs will go, but you can start with just getting them up to hip level at only halfway out. The keys are strength and flexibility.

Hurdler Stretch

Even if you can't do the splits all the way down, you will feel where you're headed. (Not being able to do the splits isn't the kiss of death, but it's a problem none the less. Practice, stretch, practice, stretch, practice, stretch, stretch, stretch…. Then do it again.

The "chair lift" will help here as well but stand parallel to the chair and steady yourself with one hand, lifting your front leg straight up. Don't be surprised if you can't lift your leg up to the proper hurdler position without any momentum, or without hunching forward and struggling. Just push as high as you can, keeping your knee straight, and pointing your toe. You will see your flexibility and your strength for what it is. Pattern the muscles in the lift and snap down. Identify which will be used to jump up and back down. When you do the jump, try to focus on using the correct muscles to move your legs into the positions required.

Watch yourself do your jumps. A mirror is great, but not always available. The bay window of your house, or a sliding glass door works great too. Close the curtains and jump outside (always check the whole area for holes and uneven ground before you start) or turn on lights and jump inside at night. The reflection will work perfectly. Watch what you're doing as you do it. This accomplishes several things. You can see what is right or wrong. You can see your height, your landing, placement of your arms and legs. Can't see it? Then you've identified your first problem! Your head should be up, back straight, eyes open and looking at the judges. If you can't see your reflection, it might be because you're looking down!

And you **MUST SMILE ALL THE TIME**. From day one. Build a habit. Feel like you're gritting your teeth and leering? That's ok. It will get less intense as you get better at the jump. Do it anyway. DON'T judge yourself. You won't be perfect as you start out. It's called practicing for a reason. The most important thing? Keep jumping. If you do the number you've set for yourself for that day… do one more. Challenge yourself to excel, and then be proud of yourself for doing it.

The proper body print for a Front Hurdler jump is to do the splits, right or left per the jump, head down on front knee, eyes on your pointed toe, candlesticks on each side of that foot. Then bend your back leg up into position.

You should find there are some different muscles involved in each position. Your butt and abs are part of the equation as well. But wait – do you feel any others? Your body will try to use whatever muscles are available to help you. Are your shoulders and arms trying to help? Let them! That's part of your prep, and a source of strength you need to tap into. Make your whole body get involved and earn their keep. NO free rides here.

Do these exercises often as you work up to your 100 jumps a day. You will find that muscles you struggled to use at first will become stronger and easier to access.

CHAPTER 8

Jumps Step by Step

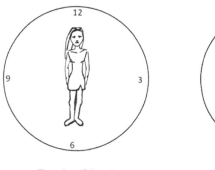

Body Clock　　　　**Floor Clock**

1. **T Jump:**

   For use as **a practice and learning jump only**. It is a learning tool and should **NEVER** be done at tryouts.

   Floor Clock: The entire jump is performed facing 6:00

   Use the "V" but when you jump, keep your legs together, straight, toes pointed. Arms stop at "T" position, like a Toe Touch as well. Do it once without putting any power behind your arms - just do the motions and let them swing into place. You will barely leave the ground. Do it again, but do the prep properly, putting the power of your arms and shoulders to work, helping your legs lift you as high as possible. The difference will surprise you. This is an excellent tool for increasing your skill at preps, and for increasing your vertical jump.

2. **Toe Touch:**

   This is the foundation jump for most cheer tryouts. It is a required jump in junior high and high school almost everywhere. The name itself is deceiving in that you don't really want to touch your toes. Think of it more as a "hand touch". Bring your feet **up** to your hands, not your hands **down** to your toes. "Reaching down" is one of the ugliest and most difficult problems to correct in jumping. Don't start the habit. Always keep your arms at shoulder height or just slightly below. Never reach down for your feet. Remember, your brain is lazy...

   Floor Clock: The entire jump is performed facing 6:00

   The proper body print for a toe touch is a straddle stretch. Keep your back straight, arms outstretched over your legs, arms in "T", hands in buckets.

Prep:

This is most important. It can be done with either type and may be different by school. Prep is usually a "V" Prep but can be Rocket done completely at 6:00 per your school's rules.

V Prep

From Prep to Jump:

The key is to use the right muscles to spring out of the prep and lift your legs to the position and height you want. To condition your muscles to lift your legs, stand with something to hold onto (a bar, the back of a chair, or even a door handle) and lift one leg to the side, angled slightly forward, and rotated so the knee faces up to the ceiling. What muscles do you feel yourself using? The top of your thigh? Your butt muscles? Embrace it and focus on lifting from there. When you do this drill, don't swing your leg up. You must lift it independently to the correct position. The help of momentum will come later once you've trained your muscles.

Get the feel of how the jump should be executed in the air by Body Printing. Sit on the floor in the straddle position. Back straight, lean slightly forward (don't hunch with rounded shoulders) and extend your arms at shoulder height over your legs. Down facing blades for hands. Close your eyes and tighten all the muscles in your body. Squeeze each section separately, focusing on how your arms feel coming out of your shoulders, how your legs feel coming out of your hips… What angle are they at? What shoulder muscles are involved with keeping the arms there? What lower back muscles are tightening to lift your legs? Lean back slightly and lift your legs. Tighten and focus. What muscles are you using? It will take more than once to get the idea. It's ok to do this every time you begin your jumps until you're successful and sure.

You must move smoothly **from Prep to Jump,** using the momentum created by bringing your arms down from the top of the prep in a circular motion in front of you, then allowing them to help lift your body into the jump position. (Remember the lift from the "T" jump exercise.) Bend your legs slightly as your arms swing by your thighs, then push off and jump!

Landing:

Recognize that returning to earth is a separate jump and you are literally pulling yourself back down. Squeeze your butt muscles and let them help pull your legs down instead of allowing them to simply fall back into place.

Get used to using the lower thigh and butt muscles when you jump back down. The leg lift is an effective exercise to build the correct muscles for jumping. You don't need to worry as much about pointed toes at this point - focus on the muscles and the lift. Obsessing too much on pointing your toes will bring your height down in the beginning. Try to build a habit of pointing, but don't let it become the main objective. Pointing your toes is worth maybe one point. Low jumps and bad landings are much more costly. Focus on height and control. Pointing is just a decision you can make later.

Landing

Land in crouch then return to ready position.

Now Put it All Together:
Start with fists on hips, then clean down sharply. Execute a strong prep, pull down hard in front, engage your arms and shoulders. For Rocket Prep, release the clasp at waist high and swing your arms out to the sides and up into position. For V prep, rotate your arms in front of your body in a wide circle, down and back up past the hips, into position. Use the full force of motion to help your legs carry you off the ground. At the same time, crouch slightly and jump hard into the air, lifting your legs up into position, then immediately reverse and jump back to the ground. Land with your feet together, in clean position, slightly crouched. Push up to standing and return to ready position, bringing your fists to your hips with a sharp, clean motion. Continue to smile at the judges until given further instructions.

Beware of the temptation to stay too long at the top. Once you've hit the jump height, reverse effort, and jump back down, keeping your knees straight until you land, then bending them slightly to allow for the needed impact cushion. Clean down and use your arms to steady yourself by tightening all your muscles and not allowing yourself to fall or step out of your landing. Clean, wait two to three beats and then perform the spiriting chosen for that jump. Always use the same spiriting for the chosen jump so it becomes second nature, allowing you to focus on showing excitement and enthusiasm instead of worrying if you will say the right thing.

3. **Front Hurdler:**

Floor Clock
(Feet @ 6:00, turning to 4:30 or 7:30, then back to 6:00)

Body Clock
(Hands and front foot @ 10:00 or 2:00)

Prep is rocket. The back leg in the turn is the front leg for the jump, therefore a left front hurdler turns to the left and uses the left leg as front, and right uses right. (Never attempt to use the other leg to "cheat" the jump with your more flexible leg. The judges will notice and reduce your score accordingly.) *Arm placement is like a rocket taking off from your chest, pulling down, around and back up. Pass the "T" mark to end with candlesticks back up where the original rocket started. Returning to the ground, your arms should sweep back down in an arc to the sides, and you will push your chest up to keep your back straighter and help your body to stay aloft longer as you jump back down.

Start at Ready Position, facing your audience. Clean. Fluid motion as you turn to the prep. Clasp as you push up to top of rocket and go to toe. Crest and pull down, using shoulders, not just arms. Do not unclasp your hands until you reach waist or hip level in front of you - your body will determine when to let go at the natural spot based on your arms and your build. From the hip, pull straight back up, lifting to the sides not straight up in front of you. Your hands will end up extended above you, turned to 10 or 2 on the **Body Clock**.

Hands are in **candlesticks**, and should be on either side of your front foot. Bring your front leg up in front, to above your head, toe pointed. Bend your back leg at the knee, tucking your back foot behind you, under your torso with a pointed toe. Hit the position, then immediately snap down legs AND arms. Be sure to lift your chest as your arms drop. Bring your arms back down to either side following the same path as they went up, **not** following your leg down in front, which would only pull you to the ground faster. Hit in slightly crouched position, arms at clean, down to the sides of your legs. Hold yourself steady, land and snap to a ready position @ 6:00, rotating back to face the crowd/judges as you hit it. Continue to smile at the judges until given further instructions.

**Remember, you must actively jump up, and jump back down. Falling out of the jump will result in a sloppy landing and an uncontrolled look to the overall trick. This is especially important in this jump. In a fluid motion, turn to your prep, right or left. As you turn, bring your arms from clean to clasp around the top of your ribcage. Immediately push up to the rocket position.

4. **Side Hurdler:**

Floor Clock
(Facing @ 6:00)

Body Clock
(Legs @ 3:00 & 9:00)

Like the Front Hurdler, this jump involves one straight and one bent leg. It is not, however, a side facing jump and the leg placement is significantly different.

This is a front facing jump. Prep can be V or Rocket. Prep instructions follow Toe Touch. Leg placement is as if you have performed a hurdler stretch in the air. Front leg is in toe touch position. Bent leg should be up, parallel to the ground, with the foot tucked behind the thigh. (In the correct position, we would be able to place a dinner plate on your bent leg and not spill the food, but close is ok.) The foot should not drag down or droop below the thigh. Arms should be in Toe Touch position, at roughly shoulder height, not reaching down. Back straight, shoulders and chest up, head up, smile and make eye contact. Landing is the same as Toe Touch. Snap down, land steady and controlled. Snap back to Ready Position and continue to smile at the judges until given further instructions.

5. **Herkie:**

Floor Clock
(Facing @ 6:00)

Body Clock
(Legs @ 4:00 & 8:00)

Like, and often mistaken for, the Side Hurdler, the Herkie is performed with less height, and with the bent knee pointed at the ground. It is **not** a recommended tryout jump. Even if the information says "Herkie", they are likely looking for a Side Hurdler. An actual Herkie is much easier, requires less flexibility, and therefore gets you less points. This jump was invented in the early years of organized cheerleading, and while it influenced all the formal jumps since, it still does not receive the respect it probably deserves. This should not be used as a tryouts jump unless you have a low skill level and no time to improve.

The prep is the same as Toe Touch - can be V Prep or Rocket Prep. The air position is like the Side Hurdler, but the bent knee will point down towards the ground, with the foot behind you, angled out away from the body, not tucked behind. Likewise, the front leg is not expected to reach hip height, as it is in a Side Hurdler, and is angled more forward as well. Traditionally, feet are meant to be cocked in this jump.

All in all, performed technically correct, it is an awkward looking jump by today's standards. But it is the founding jump of the sport and is therefore included in our breakdown.

6. **Pike Jump**:

Floor Clock
(Facing @ 6:00, turning to 3:00 or 9:00, then back to 6)

Body Clock
(Feet & hands @ 6:00)

This is the most difficult jump to get right and should only be done at tryouts if required, or if you are certain - by way of video confirmation - that your pike is perfect. If your legs slant down to the floor at all, most judges will score you low. A Pike is a vanity jump at tryouts, with many girls assuming they can get more points for a bad pike than their competition will doing an easier jump perfectly. A bad pike is still a bad jump. You will earn lower points than the perfect toe touch that went just before you. When they say to do your best jump, or "jump of choice", they don't mean "try to fool us into thinking you're better." They want you to prove it. Do **your best jump**, always.

Prep is rocket, but rotate fully to the side, at either 3:00 or 9:00. Follow the same arm directions as the Front Hurdler but bend at the waist and bring both arms to Candlesticks, extended out over both legs, which will be extended straight out from the hips. Fists and feet will both be at 3:00 on the **Body Clock**, toes must be pointed. Your arms will follow your legs straight down to the landing in this jump. Land and rotate forward as in the Front Hurdler.

Again, **do not** use this jump if it is not **perfect.**

Your position in the air **must** look as good as the picture to use this jump for tryouts. Confirm it with your own eyes by watching a video of yourself. Trust no one else's opinion. Again, this is tryouts ...

CHAPTER 9

Jumps Troubleshooting

There are many problems that can keep you from doing your best jumps. Fortunately, every problem has a solution. Here are some tips to help you correct those issues...

First and foremost, every problem, bar none, can be solved with stretching and practice. It is impossible to do the recommended 100 jumps a day and not improve. The strength and endurance achieved by doing the work will give you the height, and therefore the time during each jump, to correct problems.

1: Lack of height (Whole Body)

Do more jumps. Height comes with strength, which comes with practice. Been doing the work and you're strong, but still not getting enough height? Take a look at your prep. The prep is equally as important as the rest of the jump. Whether you're able to go to the toe, or if you are required to jump flat footed, the prep is there to assist your jump, not just to announce it. It's all about the arms, and the amount of lift you can give your body using the swing of them. Return to the section on prep and make certain you are properly executing your chosen prep. Pay close attention to form. If your prep is a rocket, firm clasp, upper arms against cheekbones, and engage your shoulders. All the muscles in your body need to be involved in the prep. Go to the toe, squeeze every muscle tight, pull down through the shoulders (not from the clasp), release the clasp at waist high, and swing hard into the T position. Allow the motion to lift you into the air. It may not seem like it, but that extra force can make a big difference.

2: Lack of Height (Legs Only)
Flexibility is key. Refer to the section on stretching and flexibility for tips. For the front hurdler, either direction, a good to excellent splits is your best friend. If you can do the splits, your leg can physically reach the necessary height to do the jump in its best form. Even if you can't, all hope is not lost. The angle of your jump to the judges is crucial to giving the illusion of height. With 12:00 at your back, and assuming the center judge is at 6:00 on the floor clock, angle your front hurdlers to 4:00-4:30 and 7:30-8:00. This angle makes the front foot look higher and allows any problems with the back foot to be hidden by the thigh. But beware! Too far to the side or front, and your jump looks awkward or clunky. (NEVER go all the way to 3:00 or 9:00)

3: Bad Landings
a: Landing with Feet Apart
Issues from lack of height to speed of jump, to "falling out of the jump" can cause this. Remember that every jump is two jumps. You jump up, then jump back down. If you don't exert enough effort in jumping down, that's falling out of the jump. It looks sloppy and results in an unstable landing. This is not only unattractive but can cause injury. Snap legs down fast and land feet together.

b: Stepping (or Falling) Out of Your Landing
This occurs when you land the jump, but aren't steady enough to keep from falling forwards, back or sideways. Jump height and speed of your jump down are key, but bending knees slightly after

you land and freezing all muscles to hold position will help as you practice the jump. Here again, arms can help. As you land and crouch slightly, back straight and chest up, press arms tightly, straight down beside your thighs, holding them together and steady to keep the lower body in place. Then pop into ready position to end the jump on solid footing. If still off balance, it may be necessary to pop into Ready At Shoulder to stabilize. Then your spiriting will provide a distraction. Always return to the Ready Position after spiriting and continue to smile at the judges while awaiting further instructions.

4: Bending Legs on the Jump Down

This is a particularly hard habit to break. It comes from trying to compensate for lack of height while learning the jumps, and results in a fear of not making the landing later. You are trying to get your legs under you because you aren't (or weren't) making your landings. Two steps to cure it… Step one is… PRACTICE!! Increase your strength, increase your height, you won't need to bend your legs! (It's a sure way to get low marks in tryouts - you must cure the habit.) Step Two is to watch your jumps! Your mind doesn't yet believe that you can get back to ground safely without bending your legs, so you have to show it. Doing jumps in front of a mirror, or a window or glass door at night, will let you see your height, and you will see that you don't really need to bend them to make your landing. Knowledge is power. Once you see it, your mind will believe it and you can kick the "leg bending" habit. This trick works with learning tumbling as well. Tell yourself out loud, "I don't need to bend my legs to land." Remember …

"What your mouth says, your ears hear, your mind believes."

TIP** No MATTER HAPPENS KEEP SMILING! Never show an error on your face! If they didn't see it but your face reacts, now they know something happened. Don't cost yourself points by not controlling your face.

CHAPTER 10

Dance & "Learn to Learn"

Material overload and inability to learn fast are two of the biggest factors in failing at tryouts. You will be required to learn at least one cheer, one chant, and a 45 to 60 second dance (it is longer than you think). Just memorizing the words to what may turn out to be the longest, least rhyming, and most awkward poem of your life is difficult at best. Combine that with three stanzas of a chant that may or may not be designed to twist your tongue and it's a lot to remember. Then there are motions for all three! It's a rough ride for the unprepared. Fortunately, you can be ready. It just takes starting in advance and "learning to learn". Find as many motions and dance moves as you can and become proficient at the execution of them. Watch videos online, watch cheers at games and learn them at home, read as many cheers as you can and memorize them. Time it. You only have 3 days to learn everything. Be sure you know how to learn the material quickly and accurately. Then you're over the biggest hurdle of the first night of clinics.

Watch and learn commonly used moves that seem easy but can be surprisingly difficult. A seated roll is easy once you've done it 50 times, but that first one is not! And the added physical need to go to the floor, execute the roll, and rise back up on beat can stress muscles you haven't used that way, resulting in soreness that hinders your performance. Better to get it over with weeks or even months in advance when it doesn't cost you points. For a trick like a roll, try it once to identify where you have trouble. You may be surprised at how difficult it is to recreate something that looks so easy! Once you've got the basics of the move down, go through it slowly and determine where you need work. Is your approach at fault, or are you weak in the muscles needed? Perhaps you need more momentum, or perhaps less. Work your way through it and even break it down into steps if necessary. Going through it from the end backwards to the beginning will often show you where you can move a foot or change the distribution of your weight to make it more efficient when going forward. You can change where you put your foot to push up to standing without changing the look of the roll. You can change rolling on the round of your butt to rolling from thigh to thigh if it works better for your body. It will look the same to others, but you will look (and feel) strong and in control of your tricks.

Jumps in the middle of cheers or dances are another pitfall, as are double jumps or optional tumbling. Practice these skills from every angle, leading with every motion you can think of.

For instance: Start out facing your left, knees bent, arms straight, with hands on knees. Now got to a toe touch. You have no break in beat from that position to your prep without being wobbly or awkward, AND you need to prep and perform a perfect jump. The key is to step to the side with your right foot, rotating to the front as you do, letting the left foot drag and snap into place as you reach the top of the prep. Arms stay straight (that's important and will require strength not to let them "flap") and go to the high V as you rotate, arriving there at the moment you hit the top of the prep, as is correct form. You must do it during the rotation using the right foot as the platform for the entire prep until the left foot catches up. Next, try it from a right facing move. Try a lunge, one arm up, the other on hip, right leg bent.

Drag your left foot to the right as you rotate front, snapping together as you reach the top and go to toe. Keep trying different moves until you can comfortably hit a solid prep from any location in a previous move. Then start adding moves. Do a whole 8 count and then hit that jump. Hit a different jump with a different prep. Once you have that down and feel you can easily hit it from any angle then look at your landings. You must also be able to go from a solid landing into a new move without looking like you fell there. Land and go left or right. Cross over your feet. Try landing from a left front hurdler and rotating to a right facing move (and look like you meant to do it). Everything you learn now will make that 3-to-4-day learning window at tryouts much easier. While others are trying to get control of landing and going to an opposing move, you will be moving on and perfecting the rest of the material because you already learned how to "land, turn, execute". One more thing to learn before you move on – the infamous 'jump coming out of a roll'. Often a roll will end by pushing up to a hurdler, meaning that you must come out of the roll strong and stable, pushing up not just to standing but right on into the rocket prep. This is the ultimate in one foot providing the whole platform for the prep. If you haven't practiced it, you may find yourself pulling a muscle. Carefully work out in advance how to safely navigate this combo. Do it multiple times slowly without the jump to learn how to navigate a safe stable prep. Only then should you add the jump. Then, if you don't need it, what have you lost? Nothing, and you have gained strength, stability, and confidence. You will go into clinics feeling like there is nothing they can throw at you that you haven't at least tried something similar to.

Knowledge is power here. **Be prepared**.

"Learn to Learn"

Give yourself 2 hours a day every day for 4 days to learn the material you've found. Find a dance online (just the dance to start – then add a cheer. Finally do cheer, chant, and dance each week.) After 2 hours, turn off the computer and continue to practice based on what you remember. You can continue to run the music to get the correct cut, but don't look at it. 2 hours a day will give you the experience of clinics and trying to remember afterwards. At the end of 4 days, you should know it perfectly. The first week, don't expect it to work perfectly. But find a new one and try again the next week. Work your way down to learning in 3 days. Then add cheer and chant material. Begin this as far ahead as possible. By tryouts, you will have taught yourself to learn a 45 to 60 second dance, a cheer, and a chant in 3 days, exactly as you will be expected to do in clinics. And a bonus is that after weeks and weeks of learning, you will have seen almost every motion combo out there. That means you are less likely to have to learn moves you've never seen before. Fewer surprises mean you can spend more time learning the words, getting everything in the right order and perfecting your delivery! And everything you practice builds strength, endurance, and confidence.

Again, knowledge is power here. Be prepared.

Remember: SMILE ALL THE TIME!!!

CHAPTER 11

Spiriting Entrance

Spiriting

As a judge for many years, I can tell you that listening to the same tired spiriting over and over at tryouts is a big turn off. The 20th times your judges hear "Let's go Bears" with a random fist pump is 19 times too many. Be original. Come up with something that will make them remember you in a good way, and then practice it until it is second nature, and you are able to put real enthusiasm behind it. Pair it with unique and engaging motions that look comfortable and natural.

Then hide it away.

NEVER share your spiriting with anyone - not a friend (even your very best friend), or a teammate, and certainly not your private coach at the local gym. That person is being paid by many hopefuls to help them "make it" and, even though they might not mean to, it may be shared with another person. If you are the second person at tryouts to do it, even if you thought of it first, you're just copying someone else. It's good to be that girl they remember. It gets you points. Be "That Girl".

Try: "Offense! Let's score!"

"Offense" – Start with one hand clasping the other wrist by your left hip, elbows bent, arms moving right and up in a round motion like an "O". Step forward (a little hop helps) with your right foot and stop your fists at the top of the "O", above your head (12:00 on the Body Clock).

"Let's Score!" – Next step forward with your left foot and hit broken T ("Let's") then punch up to hit the High V on "Score", as shown above.

*Very few will do sport specific spiriting in their entrance or after jumps. It makes you unforgettable, and shows you understand the sport.

"Hold 'em Defense!" "Toughen Up Tigers!" or "Red-and-White" (your school colors) is much better than the same old, tired rendition of "GO RED! Fired Up! Go Dogs!"

**Do not use your REAL spiriting at Mock Tryouts. Mock tryouts don't count so don't risk showing your real spiriting. Wave your arms around, yell "Go Cats!" (Or whoever) 50 times and move on. Ignore the spiriting suggestions from the outgoing cheerleaders. You have a plan. Stick to it.

NEVER YELL WHOO. It sounds like BOO when you're moving.

There are many ways to set interesting words to motions. Get creative! But keep it short, catchy, and sharp. And LOUD. Above all, be loud.

After tryouts are over, don't share it. If you do, you can't reuse it next year. If you're the only one in the room while you're doing it, then you can recycle your cute moves and sayings from year to year. If it's unique and cute enough, and if you are very memorable, you can use it next year, and the returning judges will remember you for it!

Again, try hard to be **"That Girl"**.

Entrance

Your entrance is one of the most important parts of your tryout. It's your first chance to impress the judges, and first impressions always count big!

This is where your running tumbling will go, and where your voice and spiriting make their first appearance. If you can't spirit in effectively, you miss a chance to make the judges see you as a cheerleader. Given that you will "spirit in" at every game or pep rally, they need to see that you can handle it.

Plan your tumbling carefully. You want to do your best tricks only. Never try something you are not sure of at tryouts. You are already nervous and excited. The last thing you want is to miss and fall.

If you attend a school where tumbling is not allowed, you will need to spirit in using the "Crab Steps" explained in the words and phrases section.

Go to the gym where you will tryout. Generally, the judges will sit just behind the sideline, in front of the center emblem on the gym floor. There are usually three, but occasionally four judges. You will move from the door to the center (or possibly a closer point that will be marked). Assume center until you are told otherwise. This will be discussed at tryouts, but you need to find out in advance to get comfortable with the path.

If you have tried out before, you know which doors are used. They do not generally change the process from year to year, so it is safe to assume you will enter from the same door. If you did not, then ask someone - even the coach herself - which doors you will enter and leave from, and which side of the gym the judges will be seated on. This is important because you need to learn to spirit in from that angle. Changing from right to left is harder than you think so it's important.

Once you have the layout, you can begin to plan your entrance. Ideally you will enter a door, go to the corner line of the playing floor, and tumble straight in, then move forward spiriting. This is the easiest route. Unfortunately, many gyms will be set up so that you need to angle in to get to the center spot. You can cover most of the distance via tumbling but not all. Leave room to spirit!

Count your steps! Before you go into the gym, count the number of running steps you take before tumbling. You should not be running too many steps before you start your approach to your tumbling. If so, work on cutting back. Determine how long your tumbling run is. Measure the full length of your tumbling run, including trick and landing. You can do it by dropping something as a marker at the beginning and dropping something else at the end. Go back and count the crab steps needed to cover that distance. (It's good to have someone help you here. Have someone mark the start and end over several passes. Then take the average length)

In the tryout's gym count your "Crab Steps" from the entrance door to the center. Do it three times (from each door if you're unsure as to the entrance door.) and take the average. Then measure from where your tumbling ends to the center mark. Take specific notes about the room, entrances, and the presumed location of the judges.

***Nothing is ever set in stone, so it is best to plan your entrance and then practice it from every possible angle. Arriving at tryouts to find the judges are a different place and will throw you off if you aren't ready to adjust.

Remember knowledge is power. The more you know about the facility, the fewer surprises, the less nerves. Don't worry about trying your tumbling when you're just marking the distance. Use your "Crab Steps", and later mark how far you tumble, then count how many crab steps are in that distance. You will still need to move to the spot where you will do your tryout, either by crab stepping at an angle, or by spiriting straight forward after tumbling.

When you spirit forward, you need to assume a speed that allows you to look excited, but not awkward or rushed. Straight forward is best accomplished as a few short steps, with a specific phrase and motion combination to give you purposeful steps and show confident intent. Random words or hops will look like you miscalculated or missed your ending spot. A full stop, followed by planned steps and a phrase will show that you are fully in control of your entrance and exactly where you meant to be. End with a big motion, leaning forward towards the judging table. Make eye contact with all judges individually and continue to smile. Maintain your tone and volume to the very end. You are never too close to yell, and you don't need to worry about "blowing them out". Trust me. Loud is what they live for. Give it to them.

CHAPTER 12

Floor Presence

Floor Presence is all about who you are "out there". Now, for our purposes, this will mean who you are on the tryouts floor. Not who you are in the practice room or the waiting area. It's about who you become when the time comes to perform. Dancers know it and so do actors. You can't be "on" all the time. But when it matters, you need to bring it.

Floor presence for tryouts is a combination of control and chaos. You must be sharp and intentional with your motions, but you must also bubble over with enthusiasm. The judges must see it, hear it, even feel it. Yet, it must be clear that you are in control of every motion, every jump, every step. Every move has a purpose and is finely tuned to convey your excitement and instill the same in your crowd or, for that day, the judges.

Some points to ponder:

A huge smile that never reaches your eyes is useless and flat. It's a mask, trying to hide your feelings, but an experienced judge will see right through it. Your fears, insecurities and doubts will come pouring out of your dull, unengaged eyes. You must change your mindset. You must change how you feel in order to change what you project.

To change how your mind works in tryouts you must first change your mental image of how prepared you are. This goes beyond knowing the tryouts material. This extends beyond that moment you step into the room and begin. This starts with building your signature moves and spiriting. Phrases that you will use at a variety of events when you are game spiriting later as a cheerleader. Specific movements that coincide with certain words, to tell a story. And that story is "I belong on that field".

Your confidence and consistent delivery are the foundation of your floor presence. Your excitement and attitude are the keys to making it work for you. Control and chaos in the right measures. How to find that balance? Let's start with perfecting your motions to build the foundation.

Motion Work

The accepted standard motions include such classics as High "V", Half High "V", "T", Broken T, and the Low "V" placements. There are many ways to string these together into what start as motion drills and end as spiriting sequences, they can even become a prepared piece for a cheer at camp.

The key is practice until it's perfect. Some coaches will tell you can't look natural and excited if you've memorized your spiriting. I'm here to say they are wrong. When do you feel the least nervous or inhibited? When you're in your comfort zone. Are you in your comfort zone at cheer tryouts? Not likely. You're nervous and worried you'll forget something. Maybe you're afraid you will be thrown off by someone else's mistakes – and not recover. What can you do to be as comfortable as possible? Take some of the guess work out the equation. If you have choreographed every step, motion, and word of your entrance, your after-jump spiriting, cheer, and dance spiriting, and your exit, are you still worried about what you'll say or do to make the best impression? No! You won't have to think about it. Your body will know what to do. You can trust that you will follow the known path, saying and doing the right things to the end of each spiriting. Then you can focus on putting energy behind it – punching every move hard, emphasizing each word with an energetic motion, and letting yourself go emotionally so that real excitement can show through. Confidence <u>is</u> <u>not</u> frenzy. Confidence is control. If you have one, you have the other. Then you can show some excitement without losing your focus.

Motion Drills

A good way to learn the motions is to do them in front of a mirror. Watch your arm placement. Do your arms move straight to position, strong and sharp? Or do they bounce into place, a little soft and not quite even? Don't worry - do the motions daily and watch yourself improve. Do them anytime you're able to. The more you do, the better they will get. Your arm strength increases and so does your control.

Arm strength is important to clean motions, and repeated practice is more effective than lifting weights at building the right muscles for cheer motions. **Practice really does make perfect!**

Combination and rotations – setup, repeat, commit to memory, then use as spiriting or as a cheer. Make up your own motion drills to practice.

Cheers are created by combining standard motions to create interesting routines. Expect to see unusual and often awkward motion sets in tryouts routines. They will try to confuse you, so practice until your motions are second nature. Your arms hit the right placement without thinking about it. Make sure that you continue to practice any groundwork such as seat rolls or going to your knees and back up smoothly while doing the motions. Then, no matter what they put in the routines, you can already do it and focus on learning the sequence, not the motions.

> **TIP**** This is where Learn to Learn comes in! Once you've learned several dances, you'll find you are mostly using the same motions and moves again and again. They become familiar - second nature. You know how to go into a seat roll or turn on your knees and get back up gracefully, without sacrificing any power. Again, most of your competition will be learning to do it that week. You're already way ahead.

Spiriting Drills

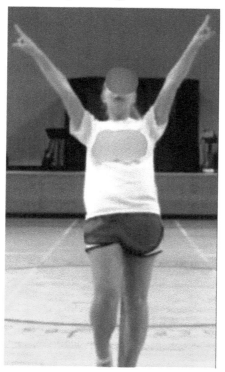

Start at ready, then clean (you can return to this position at any time, from any position, and look natural).

Steps 1-4:

1. Step forward – right foot only – High "V" (keep your weight on your left foot)

2. Shift weight to forward (right) foot, drag your left toe, and pull down to Table Tops (lift your chest and push your hips slightly forward).

3. Step together into a crouch, pull down to Low Touchdown

4. Pop out to feet apart, left hand on hip – bring right fist straight up in front of your body ending at Half High "V". * Hit it all at same time, so that right arm has to move fast (Do not bend your elbow – This is a sweep not a punch.)

You have just completed your first "spiriting sequence" for after a jump, skill, or cheer.

Now add words. Don't try to do a word per move. It's more natural to let it flow.

Try "Blue" on Step 1.

Then add "and White!" at 3 and 4.

Drop your chin slightly on 3 but do not break eye contact with your judges / audience. Snap your head back up with your right arm to emphasize the ending. Return to ready position after.

   "Wat-kins"   x (clap)   **"Tig-ers"**
(by 8 count)
The Watkins is the 1-2 (broken High V to High V – makes a W)
The Clap is 3 (back in front of your chest)
The Tigers hits 4-5 (broken T to T –Tigers – lift your chin on -gers)
Nod 6 (easier from a slightly lifted chin), Hold 7, Clean 8
Back to Ready Position.
based on the common 8 count.

Do it enough times that you have the moves/words down. (You can insert your team if it works – change it if not – "Ross Rams" will work differently
hit Ross at High "V" 1_ pause
pull Table Tops then punch down to low touchdown – 2-3,

sweep to "Rams" at Half High "V" on 4 right arm, step forward right foot.
lift chin on 5, nod on 6, hold on 7, Clean on 8.

Once you've got it down do it in the mirror – Don't just try to video / watch / video – it's too slow. If not mirror, find a big window (make sure no one is inside.) Do it over and over. Watch your body. From move to move – do your arms look right? Shoulders engaged" (Yes, you'll see it.) Do you coil and spring from crouch to pop out? Are you punching the motions? Is the timing, right? What if it's not working for you? Tweak it! You can stay at Half High V but punch it slightly forward at the judges. Or still sweep up to the Half High V, but with a two-step charge to the judges. Or instead of Popping Out, jump back with your lower half only (feet together, slightly on toes, bootie pushed out behind, top half leaning forward. This is a less stable ending, and you need to recover quickly by dropping your heels and hitting clean before you lose your balance.

Floor Presence is all about intentional enthusiasm and controlling your presentation. Solid motions in planned sequences are your firm foundation.

Changing your level of preparedness will directly affect how you react to stress – if you feel prepared and you know that you know the material, you will be less nervous. When you step out on the floor you can focus on performing instead of remembering.

Learning to learn is the key – knowing that you are fully prepared gives you a sense of calm.

When you have prepared yourself - when you know your jumps are great and your skills are on point - then you can relax and focus on projecting excitement and bringing the spirit. You can focus on putting on a show!

Attitude

Gotta' breakout the attitude.

Floor presence it may seem cocky, but once you've done the work, you've got the collateral to back it up.

You need to be watching videos of those whose presence you want to embody. Watch online videos of college games and competitions. Watch high schools – watch your own high school's videos – look for the attitude you want and recreate it – without any weird facials, of course.

Watch videos from cheer camps if you can find them. Instructors at camp know this part cold. They are doing the same cheers and dances every week all summer. They know how to turn on the attitude and create good floor presence when they'd rather be sunbathing. You can do the same. You practice the motions until you've got it so cold you can do it without thinking about it – then focus on bringing that <u>attitude!</u>

CHAPTER 13

Tumbling

Tumbling is critical to attaining a position on a Varsity squad in most high schools across America these days. While you may be able to make a team without it, you will likely be relegated to the "non tumbler" field positions (either the inconvenient stunt done while others tumble, or that "walk through" person who either moves position, continues to do motions, or fakes a tumbling trick while others actually do it. None of these are ideal, and for tryouts, it can be the thing that drops you out of a team. Tumbling points are typically higher than jumps and other skills. A well scored Round Off Back Handspring can beat a competitor's better dance or cheer score easily, especially if the tumbler has a decent score in the same alternate skill. In tryouts, points rule. If you don't have tumbling, you must be hands down the very best at everything else. That's a tough order given the number of other avenues for points. Better to bite the bullet and learn to tumble. All gyms, and many dance companies, have beginner classes designed for those needing basic skills to achieve a goal. It is not necessary to pay for private lessons, although it is faster.

Be sure to practice tumbling on a wood floor, or at least on the "hard floor" at your tumbling gym. If you don't have access to a one at your tumbling gym, try to get time to practice on a wood gym floor either at a local school, or possibly at a church. Be certain the floor is smooth and relatively dust free before you begin. Broken or warped boards can be dangerous, and heavy dust or wax build up can result in a slippery surface. It is important that you do not go from a spring floor to tryouts on a wood floor without first practicing, as the difference in your rebound and height will be significant at first.

Cartwheel, Round Off, Standing Back Handspring, Round Off Back Handspring, Round Off Back Tuck, and Standing Back Tuck are the base tumbling skills most often seen in high school tryouts, in order of difficulty. Higher skills may or may not be allowed, based on the coach and school or district rules. Some advanced tumbling is not recommended for wood floors and would therefore not be allowed. Ask for limits at the pre-tryouts meeting.

Tumbling Troubleshooting

To learn tumbling skills, you should look for qualified instructors teaching in equipped gyms. Most cheer and tumbling gyms will offer a beginning tumbling class to teach you the basics.

1: Fear of Failure in Tumbling Class:

If you arrive and you're the oldest (sometimes by several years) or even just the "furthest behind", don't be discouraged! You need this skill, and you're doing the work to get it. If there is an alternate class you can take with others more your age or skill level, that's fine. If not, stick to it! Younger girls will learn faster because they are closer to the ground, usually more flexible and have fewer female curves to throw off their center of balance. Most importantly, they haven't learned the fear that you have at an older age. Fear will stop you from achieving your dream if you let it, so don't be afraid of those little girls! Go to class, encourage them, and let them encourage you! Your instructor will teach you differently based on your ability and body type - go with it! Do your best and work hard!

2: Fear of Not Having a Spotter:

When you're doing a back handspring (flip flop, whatever they call it in your area), if you only need a very light spot (or really no spot at all) but you're afraid to do it alone, have someone video you. Watch the video and you can see that the spotter isn't helping you at all! Once you see yourself doing it without help, you'll be more confident in doing it completely alone. Your eyes don't lie! AND the instructor WILL NOT encourage you to do it alone if they aren't completely confident that you can. They are adults with jobs who can be fired or sued if you get hurt because they didn't help you when needed. They will not risk you getting injured. Go for it!!

3: Fear of "Dropping Yourself":
Do not do this exercise without a qualified spotter who can hold you as needed. As with all suggestions, attempt at your own risk.

You know you can do it, and you have done it, but you feel like your arms might give out and let your head hit the floor? Work on your arm and shoulder strength!

Inverted pushups against the wall can help. Find a safe spot where you can do a handstand against the wall, and no one will come around the corner and run into you. You also want enough room around you that you won't hit something when you come down or if you slide to either side. Start with white socks (Someone will be upset if you mark up the wall with shoes or dirty feet.) Do a handstand about 8-10" from the base of the wall and let your back arch slightly so that your toes are touching the wall. Find a spotter who can support you until you are sure of your strength and ability to hold yourself up. It is best to have someone catch your feet and let you get settled against the wall the first few times. Once you're comfortable, very carefully bend your elbows just a bit and immediately straighten them again. You should be able to feel your level of strength and know if you can try a little deeper bend. *DO NOT bend them all the way!! If you do, you will be surprised when you really do hit your head on the floor! And DO NOT arch your neck and look back at the wall. Look straight forward, out into the room in the position you will be in when you tumble. * You won't be able to do more than one or two at first, and you will find that your arms and shoulders will be sore later but keep doing it every day! It will pay off, both in strength and confidence. Not only will your arms and shoulders get stronger in that position, but you will KNOW they are. That counts for as much or more than anything.

CHAPTER 14

Clinic Week

As you read at the beginning of this book, Tryouts is an audition, and you are trying to win a part.

Tryouts consist of four parts:

1. Tryouts Meeting - mandatory w/parent or guardian – usually a few weeks prior to Tryouts to discuss requirements in grades, cost, & commitment. Forms will be handed out and timelines for returning them established. Do Not Miss The Deadlines.

2. Clinic Week (usually 3 days – bring clothes, shoes, something to put your hair up and water)

3. Mock Tryouts (usually day before tryouts)

4. Tryouts (last day – you will be told the rules – can someone be with you? Can you bring food? How long should it take?)

Clinics are usually 2-3 hour long sessions where you are given information about how tryouts will be done, how you will be scored, and you will be taught the tryouts material. They may ask you to bring your tryouts clothes to be approved. If you must, fold them neatly in a clean bag and fold them back into it neatly after. They must be pristine on tryouts day.

You will also draw your number for tryouts order. This will determine what group you try out with for all or part of the material. **This is important. ** If you try out with someone who isn't good, their mistakes can throw you off so you will need to be able to stay on beat. This is still good because the judges will see that you can keep going no matter what happens in a game or routine. Likewise, if you are trying out with the best person in the room, that's a plus! They will stay on the beat and not throw you off! And if you're the first person to tryout – SCORE! The judges have no preconceived notions about what they are going to see. You are setting the baseline! But being last is great as well since every judge waits for "That Girl" (or Boy). On the last person, they are tired of all the "Whoo's" and the same, dull spiriting. Your fresh material and enthusiasm will bring them back to life and they will love you!

Generally, you will not be allowed to record the material taught. Some schools will give you a printout of the words to cheer and chant. (Make sure you have a pen and paper in your bag and write them down during break if they don't.) Most of them will give you a way to access the dance music for practice (probably a link). All will teach by standing in front of you, facing away, expecting you to follow along. Usually there will be several outgoing cheerleaders around the room to show motions and the front person should turn frequently to show motions from the front. You will be in a big room or gym with all the other hopefuls – make sure you can see and hear. If your best friend likes to giggle and chat, tell them in advance you'll be focused and may move away to be able to hear and see better. Let them know you need them to understand you will talk later. *Clinics are also a time for the coach to watch who is paying attention and who will be an asset to the team. While they don't usually get a say in the scoring, it will set the tone for your relationship with them. If your friends aren't serious about doing their best, tell them you will see them after tryouts.

Find tryouts buddies to practice with after clinics every night. EVERY NIGHT. Offer to get pizza so everyone can stay together and keep working. Run the music over and over, do the chant 100 times, do the cheer until you hate it but it's perfect. Still guard your spiriting though! Practice that privately. Remember – if someone does it before you, it's old news.

Talk to your family well ahead of that week. Remind them you've been working for months to get to this. Things like Grandma's birthday dinner could be done the day after tryouts or the weekend prior. Believe me, she's more interested in seeing you happy and successful than hearing you sing happy birthday ON TUESDAY. Plan for your schoolwork so you don't have much to do that week. This may require working to get ahead – if your teacher usually assigns a random section of the book questions for homework, do the lesson the weekend before and work ALL the questions. That way you've already done the homework no matter what section is chosen. Ask for handouts in advance or about quizzes/tests. Let your teacher know you are participating in tryouts and that you'd like to be ready for class in advance because it will be a busy and stressful week. If they aren't interested in helping you, then get busy and learn that week's material on your own. No excuses. Just make it happen. You won't have time for hours of homework so work hard all year to be on point with your studies, then work ahead to be on point that week.

Mock Tryouts

Mock Tryouts is a practice tryout, usually held on the last day of clinics. You will go through the tryout material, from start to finish, just as you will perform it at real tryouts, although you won't usually be in the gym with just your group. Usually, the judges are the current seniors, and maybe the coaches. They will give you a "score sheet" filled with helpful hints – maybe. Take the constructive hints and leave the rest. Some of these mock judges may be interested in helping their friends make the squad and they may or may not have your best interest at heart. Use the Mock Tryout as your own planning session. Does my entrance fit? Can I make it to the proper spot before I run out of spiriting? DO NOT use your real spiriting at Mock Tryouts!! This is a prime opportunity for someone to hear it and tell it to their friend. You need them to tell you if you don't smile, or you look nervous. You need them to tell you if you're behind on the dance beat or missing motions. At this stage of your training, you will know how you did. You don't need their opinion on your ability. And you don't need their opinion on your spiriting. Wave your arms around and yell "Go Dogs!" 50 times! They will tell you to use more spiriting choices at tryouts. And you will!

CHAPTER 15

Your Time to Shine

TRYOUTS DAY! It's finally here and if you've put in the work, you're ready!

Eat a light breakfast and lunch that day — nothing spicy or rich. Plan to have someone bring you a dinner that is light, easy to eat, and NOT MESSY. Take no chances. But eat it! Tryouts can take hours and you don't want to be sick.

Head to the gym immediately after classes and get changed. Do your hair and make sure you're ready. Then stretch and start running through the material. Everyone else will be doing the same. Often, they will play the dance music every 5 min over speakers in the waiting area. Keep stretching and practicing until it's your turn. While you need to be kind, don't get involved in the drama and nerves of others. It will only bring you down and destroy your chances. Some people decompress by falling apart, and some need to hear reinforcement. You can do that after you've done your tryout. Until then, stay away from them. And don't hug!! Mascara on your shirt isn't going to help the person who is upset. Hug them after the results come out. You need to stay clean and ready until any callbacks are announced.

Callbacks are done if there are ties in scores, if one judge forgot to score a certain part or if two judges gave drastically different scores for the same hopeful. It must be assumed that one was looking at the wrong person and the participant will be asked to tryout again. Sometimes it will be only two people who are in question but usually a full set of three will be asked back. This doesn't mean the people asked back are "in the bottom". Often a participant will be asked back with others to round out the numbers and to reset a baseline. You will do the whole routine again.

CHAPTER 16

The End Result

Depending on the program, you will either receive a letter after try-outs, or the results will be posted in some way. Some programs even make you wait until the next day. When you get your results, be gracious either way.

If you made it, be kind to those who didn't and sincere when thanking others who congratulate you. Your attitude will set the tone for your ongoing relationships with others who tried out.

If you did not make it, be gracious and congratulate those who did. Even if you think the scoring was wrong and someone made it who shouldn't have, be gracious and kind. Take your tears home and share them with those closest to you. Again, your attitude will set the tone for your continued relationships with others who tried out. And sometimes things change, and you get called up because someone had to leave the squad. If you have complained or accused, it will be a very uncomfortable year... for you.

If you didn't make it, look honestly at your attempt. Were you ready? Did you freeze? Mess up? Didn't have your skills at a the right level? Reset your goals and get back to work.

Cheering just one year is better than not trying again. Don't quit working! And maybe tryout for mascot this year? It's a great way to be part of the team, make friends and learn a lot about cheer.

If you made it – Congratulations! Now get back to work! Camp and football season will be here before you know it! You never want to be the worst cheerleader on the squad. Don't quit working. When those who didn't make it look at the squad, you want to be sure they never look at you as the one who shouldn't be there. (And they **will** look.) Always do the best you can so you can be proud of the spot you worked so hard for. And remember, if you're not a senior, tryouts will be here again before you know it! Go back to page one and do it again! There is always room for improvement. Always.

CHAPTER 17

Training Plans and Timelines

1: 12 Month Plan

2: 9 Month Plan

3: 6 Month Plan

4: 3 Month Plan

5. 1 Month Plan

12 Month Plan (12 Months to Tryouts)

1ˢᵗ – 3 months (Phase 1)

If you have 12 months until tryouts, follow this plan!

For 12 months down to 9 months

Chapter 5: Motions

Chapter 6: Jumps - What Are They?

Chapter 7: Before you Jump

Chapter 8: Jumps Step by Steps

Chapter 9: Jumps Troubleshooting

Chapter 10: Dance - Learn to Learn

Chapter 13: Tumbling

Move on to 2ⁿᵈ – 3 months (Phase 2)

12 Month Plan (9 Months to Tryouts)

2nd – 3 months (Phase 2)

Now you're 9 months from tryouts! Keep working the plan!

For 9 months down to 6 months

Chapter 2: Words and Phrases

Chapter 8: Jumps Step by Steps

Chapter 9: Jumps Troubleshooting

Chapter 10: Dance - Learn to Learn

Chapter 12: Floor Presence

Move on to 3rd – 3 months (Phase 3)

12 Month Plan (6 Months to Tryouts)

3rd – 3 months (Phase 3)

Now you're 6 months from tryouts! Keep working the plan!

For 6 months down to 3 months

Chapter 5: Motions

Chapter 10: Dance - Learn to Learn

Chapter 11: Spiriting Entrance

Move on to 3 Months (Phase 4)

12 Month Plan (3 Months to Tryouts)

3 months (Phase 4)

Now you're 3 months from tryouts! Keep working the plan!

For 3 months down to 1 month

Chapter 4: Dress for Success

Chapter 10: Dance - Learn to Learn

Chapter 14: Clinic Week

Move on to 1 Month (Phase 5)

12 Month Plan (1 Month to Tryouts)

1 Month (Phase 5)

Now you're 1 month from tryouts! Kick it into gear!

Chapter 11: Spiriting Entrance

Chapter 14: Clinic Week

Chapter 15: Your Time to Shine

Chapter 16: The End Result

GOOD LUCK! YOU GOT THIS!!

9 Month Plan (9 Months to Tryouts)

1st – 3 months (Phase 1)

If you have 9 months until tryouts, follow this plan!

For 9 months down to 6 months

Chapter 2: Words and Phrases

Chapter 5: Motions

Chapter 6: Jumps - What Are They?

Chapter 7: Before you Jump

Chapter 8: Jumps Step by Steps

Chapter 9: Jumps Troubleshooting

Chapter 10: Dance - Learn to Learn

Chapter 13: Tumbling

Move on to 2nd – 3 months (Phase 2)

9 Month Plan (6 Months to Tryouts)

2nd – 3 months (Phase 2)

Now you're 6 months from tryouts! Keep working the plan!

For 6 months down to 3 months

Chapter 8: Jumps Step by Steps

Chapter 9: Jumps Troubleshooting

Chapter 10: Dance - Learn to Learn

Chapter 12: Floor Presence

Move on to 3 months (Phase 3)

9 Month Plan (3 Months to Tryouts)

3 months (Phase 3)

Now you're 3 months from tryouts! Keep working the plan!

For 3 months down to 1 month

Chapter 4: Dress for Success

Chapter 10: Dance - Learn to Learn

Chapter 14: Clinic Week

Move on to 1 Month (Phase 4)

9 Month Plan (1 Month to Tryouts)

1 month (Phase 4)

Now you're 1 month from tryouts! Kick it into gear!

Chapter 11: Spiriting Entrance

Chapter 14: Clinic Week

Chapter 15: Your Time to Shine

Chapter 16: The End Result

GOOD LUCK! YOU GOT THIS!

6 Month Plan (6 Months to Tryouts)

1st – 3 months (Phase 1)

If you have 6 months until tryouts, follow this plan!

For 6 months down to 3 months

Chapter 2: Words and Phrases

Chapter 5: Motions

Chapter 6: Jumps - What Are They?

Chapter 7: Before you Jump

Chapter 8: Jumps Step by Steps

Chapter 9: Jumps Troubleshooting

Chapter 10: Dance - Learn to Learn

Chapter 12: Floor Presence

Chapter 13: Tumbling

Move on to 3 months (Phase 2)

6 Month Plan (3 Months to Tryouts)

3 months (Phase 2)

Now you're 3 months from tryouts! Keep working the plan!

For 3 months down to 2 months

Chapter 8: Jumps Step by Steps

Chapter 9: Jumps Troubleshooting

Chapter 10: Dance - Learn to Learn

Chapter 11: Spiriting Entrance

Chapter 12: Floor Presence

Move on to 2 months (Phase 3)

6 Month Plan (2 Months to Tryouts)

2 months (Phase 3)

Now you're 2 months from tryouts! Keep working the plan!

For 2 months down to 1 month

Chapter 4: Dress for Success

Chapter 10: Dance - Learn to Learn

Chapter 14: Clinic Week

Move on to 1 Month (Phase 4)

6 Month Plan (1 Month to Tryouts)

1 Month (Phase 4)

Now you're 1 month from tryouts! Kick it into gear!

Chapter 11: Spiriting Entrance

Chapter 14: Clinic Week

Chapter 15: Your Time to Shine

Chapter 16: The End Result

GOOD LUCK! YOU GOT THIS!

3 Month Plan (3 Months to Tryouts)

3 months (Phase 1)

If you have 3 months until tryouts, follow this plan!

For 3 months down to 2 months

Chapter 2: Words and Phrases

Chapter 5: Motions

Chapter 6: Jumps - What Are They?

Chapter 7: Before you Jump

Chapter 8: Jumps Step by Steps

Chapter 9: Jumps Troubleshooting

Chapter 10: Dance - Learn to Learn

Chapter 12: Floor Presence

Chapter 13: Tumbling

Move on to 2 months (Phase 2)

3 Month Plan (2 Months to Tryouts)

2 months (Phase 2)

Now you're 2 months from tryouts! Keep working the plan!

For 2 months down to 1 month

Chapter 4: Dress for Success

Chapter 8: Jumps Step by Steps

Chapter 9: Jumps Troubleshooting

Chapter 10: Dance - Learn to Learn

Chapter 11: Spiriting Entrance

Chapter 12: Floor Presence

Move on to 1 month (Phase 3)

3 Month Plan (1 Month to Tryouts)

1 Month (Phase 3)

Now you're 1 month from tryouts! Keep working the plan!

For 1 month down to 2 weeks

Chapter 5: Motions

Chapter 10: Dance - Learn to Learn

Chapter 11: Spiriting Entrance

Chapter 14: Clinic Week

Move to 2 Weeks (Phase 4)

3 Month Plan (2 Weeks to Tryouts)

2 weeks (Phase 4)

Now you're 2 weeks from tryouts! Keep working the plan!

For 2 weeks down to 1 week

Chapter 10: Dance - Learn to Learn

Chapter 14: Clinic Week

Chapter 15: Your Time to Shine

Chapter 16: The End Result

Move on to 1 Week (Phase 5)

3 Month Plan (1 Week to Tryouts)

1 Week (Phase 5)

Now you're 1 week from tryouts! Kick it into gear!

Chapter 14: Clinic Week

Chapter 15: Your Time to Shine

Chapter 16: The End Result

GOOD LUCK! YOU GOT THIS!

1 Month Plan (1 Months to Tryouts)

4 Weeks to Tryouts (Phase 1)

If you have 4 weeks until tryouts, follow this plan!

For 4 weeks down to 3 weeks

Chapter 2: Words and Phrases

Chapter 4: Dress for Success

Chapter 5: Motions

Chapter 6: Jumps - What Are They?

Chapter 7: Before you Jump

Chapter 8: Jumps Step by Steps

Chapter 9: Jumps Troubleshooting

Chapter 10: Dance - Learn to Learn

Chapter 12: Floor Presence

Chapter 13: Tumbling

Move on to 3 Weeks (Phase 2)

I Month Plan (3 Weeks to Tryouts)

3 Weeks to Tryouts (Phase 2)

Now you're 3 weeks from tryouts! Keep working the plan!

For 3 weeks down to 2 weeks

Chapter 5: Motions

Chapter 10: Dance - Learn to Learn

Chapter 11: Spiriting Entrance

Move on to 2 Weeks (Phase 3)

I Month Plan (2 weeks to Tryouts)

2 Weeks (Phase 3)

Now you're 2 weeks from tryouts! Keep working the plan!

For 2 weeks down to I week

Chapter II: Spiriting Entrance

Chapter 12: Floor Presence

Chapter 14: Clinic Week

Chapter 15: Your Time to Shine

Chapter 16: The End Result

Move on to I Week (Phase 4)

1 Month Plan (1 Week to Tryouts)

1 Week to Tryouts (Phase 4)

Now you're 1 week from tryouts! Kick it into gear!

Chapter 14: Clinic Week

Chapter 15: Your Time to Shine

Chapter 16: The End Result

GOOD LUCK! YOU GOT THIS!

Printed in the USA
CPSIA information can be obtained
at www.ICGtesting.com
LVHW011043271023
762204LV00019B/699